C000129896

PENGUIN
SPECIALS

Penguin Specials fill a gap. Written by some of today's most exciting and insightful writers, they are short enough to be read in a single sitting – when you're stuck on a train; in your lunch hour; between dinner and bedtime. Specials can provide a thought-provoking opinion, a primer to bring you up to date, or a striking piece of fiction. They are concise, original and affordable.

To browse digital and print Penguin Specials titles, please refer to **www.penguin.com.au/penguinspecials**

Generation HK

Seeking Identity in China's Shadow

BEN BLAND

PENGUIN BOOKS

UK | USA | Canada | Ireland | Australia
India | New Zealand | South Africa | China

Penguin Books is part of the Penguin Random House group of companies
whose addresses can be found at global.penguinrandomhouse.com

First published by Penguin Group (Australia) 2017

3 5 7 9 10 8 6 4 2

Cover photography © Antony Dapiran
Cover design by Di Suo © Penguin Group (Australia)
Text design by Steffan Leyshon-Jones © Penguin Group (Australia)
Printed and bound in Hong Kong by Printing Express

penguin.com.au

ISBN: 9780734398505

CONTENTS

'Wherever there is oppression, there is resistance.'

Zhou Enlai, Chinese premier
Shanghai, 1972

Preface

When I moved to Hong Kong in early 2015, I feared that I had missed all the action. Foreign correspondents live on drama, and by then it seemed as if it was all over, except for a few sorry-looking tents and protesters outside the city's Legislative Council.

The Occupy movement had stirred more than 100000 people to take to the streets, brought swathes of the city centre to a standstill for weeks and thrust Hong Kong's struggle for democracy against an uncompromising Chinese government into the global spotlight. The Umbrella Revolution – as it was also known after the umbrellas that demonstrators used to fend off pepper spray fired by the police – had ended with seemingly little change. The solidarity that had brought parents out to defend their children and others' from the perceived brutality of the police, the carnival atmosphere generated by artists trying to lift up the thousands sleeping in tents and the sense of unity in purpose. None of it could – or would – last.

In a fast-moving, crowded city, more and more Hong Kongers became frustrated with the road closures in the important business and shopping districts of Admiralty, Causeway Bay and Mong Kok. Youth leaders split from their adult counterparts once they realised that occupying the streets would not force China's Communist leaders to give semi-autonomous Hong Kong the right to choose its own leader in a genuinely democratic election. Students argued among themselves over calls for more violent action.

By early 2015, prominent Occupy leaders like Joshua Wong were feeling downhearted. Despite the powerful force they created, they failed to achieve their goals. They could see no way forward in the face of an autocratic Chinese government that would never grant such concessions to people they viewed as illegal protesters. Yet, although it was not obvious at the time, Occupy would prove to be a potent fertiliser for the seeds of generational change that were already sprouting in Hong Kong.

Over the next eighteen months, I watched with amazement as Hong Kong was swept by a wave of political change that no-one had predicted. Disappointment at the failure to win democratic elections hardened into a growing rejection of Beijing's rule over Hong Kong. China's secretive government responded by dramatically intensifying its interventions in the affairs of semi-autonomous Hong Kong, kidnapping booksellers, interfering in the political process, and leaning on its allies in the territory to enhance censorship and close down public debate.

In light of this, Wong founded a political party to fight for office with his friends Agnes Chow and Nathan Law. Other students who had earned their political spurs during Occupy reacted strongly against these advocates of peaceful civil disobedience and gradual change, calling for full independence from China and violent opposition to the authorities. Increasingly alarmed by this separatism, the Beijing and Hong Kong governments stepped up their repression, which backfired as Hong Kongers resisted using the unique freedoms they still had available.

The Umbrella movement grabbed so much attention in Hong Kong and beyond because it rudely upended the casual stereotypes about this city of 7 million people. A Great Mall of China, where people were more interested in buying the latest designer handbag or Hello Kitty accessory than fighting for political and social change. The truth was, as always, far more complex. Since the British took control of Hong Kong in 1841, the city has had a turbulent history of boycotts, protests and riots.

Before the handover to Chinese control in 1997, many of these actions were targeted against the British colonial authorities. Since then, the focus of protests has shifted to the Chinese government and Hong Kongers' struggle to obtain democracy and maintain their autonomy. In that sense, the Umbrella movement was the culmination of previous upheavals. Young Hong Kongers wanted change and they wanted it now.

Arguably, the huge crowds during Occupy, and the radicalisation that has taken place since, were partly driven by economics. As a gateway port, Hong Kong thrived when China opened up its economy from the late 1970s onwards. Still, as in many nations, the financial benefits went to the baby boomers. Their children and grandchildren have been saddled with the world's highest property prices, relative to salaries. When graduate earnings have not increased for years and the younger generations have to put off marriage because they cannot afford even a 15 square metre flat, it is natural for them to express frustration towards the government. More so when it is of the puppet variety, appointed by rulers distant in geography and mindset.

Change has also been driven by the Newtonian nature of politics, where every repressive action by the government was met with an opposing force by democracy campaigners, and vice versa. But as I spent more time talking to young people, I realised that there were deeper forces at play.

At one anti-Beijing protest, I met a group of young people who were waving Hong Kong's old British colonial flag, an unimaginable act in the other former Western colonies where I had lived, like Indonesia, Singapore and Vietnam. More perplexingly, when I went to ask them why they were doing this, I discovered that they could barely speak English. The flag, they told me in halting English, was a symbol of their rejection of Chinese rule and desire for an independent Hong Kong, rather than for the return of their British overlords.

A whole generation came of age in the twenty years since Hong Kong was handed back to Chinese control by Britain in 1997. This cohort, which I call Generation HK, is unique. Unlike their parents and grandparents, they are not bound by the traditions and limitations of British colonial rule. They also have much weaker ties to the Mainland than their ancestors, many of whom fled poverty and political repression in Communist China for the relative safety and prosperity of Hong Kong. Caught between two worlds, these young Hong Kongers are struggling to define themselves and their future at a time of increasing uncertainty.

Behind the façades of towering skyscrapers, teeming malls and thronged restaurants, Hong Kong feels to me like a place that is uncomfortable with its history, unhappy with its present and unsure of its future. On the political front, young Hong Kongers are fighting to defend the democratic freedoms that were guaranteed on paper by Beijing for fifty years from 1997. The clock is ticking, with only thirty years left. On the economic front, they are fighting to survive in one of the world's most expensive and imbalanced cities, where transient foreign bankers and lawyers live the high life alongside the local elite, while the rest struggle to get by. On the social front, they are fighting to forge their own identity in a city where the pressure from parents and society to marry early and seek material wealth remains strong. An emboldened Generation HK has exposed the underlying contradictions of the 'One Country, Two Systems' arrangement under which Hong Kong returned to Chinese control. It is now being tested to its limits.

'One Country, Two Systems' was a compromise designed to assuage the fears of Hong Kong people that they would be simply subsumed into China on 1 July 1997 – and stop them fleeing en masse. The Basic Law, the mini-constitution that came into force after the handover, states that Hong Kong will be given a 'high degree of autonomy'. That it will have power over everything apart from defence and foreign affairs and that the freedoms of speech, assembly and protest will be guaranteed. Hong Kongers' 'way of life shall remain unchanged for 50 years,' they were promised. But the Basic Law also said that Beijing had the power to appoint the territory's leader – known as the chief executive – as well as other senior officials. It required Hong Kong to implement a draconian security law against 'treason, secession, sedition, subversion', the sort of vague offences used to jail human rights lawyers, environmental activists and other critics in President Xi Jinping's China. And, crucially, China's rubber-stamp parliament, known as the National People's Congress, had the ultimate power to interpret the Basic Law, despite the judicial independence promised to Hong Kong on paper.

In the early years after the handover, the inherent contradictions of 'One Country, Two Systems' were more easily papered over. Hong Kong's baby boomers, who had a stronger affinity for the Mainland, profited handsomely from China's fast-growing economy, while a previous generation of Communist leaders in Beijing took a softer approach to Hong Kong. Yet, young Hong Kongers feel they have missed out on the benefits of the long economic boom, while experiencing the negative side-effects of over-crowding and sky-high property prices.

Even then, this isn't the end to Generation HK's problems. As the political, social and economic realities around them change, they face a wider struggle to redefine their identity. In Europe and the US, enterprising university students are rushing to sign up for Mandarin classes and fighting each other for prized internships in Beijing or Shanghai. Members of Generation HK see the promotion of Mandarin as a threat to their Cantonese dialect and are rebelling against the growing use of the Mainland's 'simplified' Chinese characters instead of the more complex and 'traditional' ones they learnt as children. Officials in the Chinese and Hong Kong government like to say that young people have become carried away with 'Two Systems' and forget that they are part of 'One Country'. But, for Generation HK, forging their own way in the world is about more than simply opposing the Chinese government.

Captivated by the contradictions of Hong Kong and curious about the direction of the tectonic plates shifting underneath the surface, I embarked on a journey to find out about the hopes and fears of this generation. There were burning questions in my mind. What is it like to grow up in a city that is meant to enjoy Western-style democratic freedoms while being brought ever closer into the embrace of one of the world's most powerful authoritarian states? How do you define yourself when you are ethnically Chinese but have no love for the Chinese state that you feel threatens your way of life? How do you get ahead when it seems that many of the best opportunities were locked down by previous generations?

I started my quest in the most obvious place, going to talk to former Occupy leaders like Joshua Wong, Agnes

Chow and Nathan Law as they battled their way out of despair and regrouped for the next fight. Wong had first come to public attention when he led a successful campaign against plans to bring in a Communist-style Moral and National Education system in 2011 and 2012. For many young Hong Kongers, it was their first taste of politics, on the streets or otherwise.

From there, I decided to look at the wider problems facing the education system, which was the root of many frustrations felt by young people. The bizarre phenomenon of celebrity super tutors, a category peculiar to Hong Kong, was the perfect lens with which to peer more deeply into the field of education. Intense parental pressure and a rigid exam-driven system that favours rote-learning over a broader quest for knowledge leave many Hong Kong pupils tired and stressed. But some industrious individuals saw in this problem an opportunity and built careers as highly successful private tutors. These young after-school teachers of everything, from Chinese to Mathematics, can earn hundreds of thousands or even millions of US dollars. Idolised by fans, with K-pop hair and fancy cars, their images can be seen on billboards across town. YY Lam – the best-known and best-paid of the celebrity tutors – embodied the contradictions facing Generation HK. The 28-year-old had an inspiring back-story, having worked his way up from humble beginnings to multi-millionaire status thanks to his mastery of Chinese literature and his enthusiasm for teaching. Even then, he still acknowledged that his success was only possible because of the big problems with the system.

In hierarchical Hong Kong, exams are designed to funnel the brightest to university and thence to the establishment professions like law, accountancy and medicine, where plentiful money can be made by those who do not rock the boat. For Generation HK, the expectation that with power comes the responsibility to keep your mouth shut was changing. I went to talk to three young professionals who were pushing back and defying convention. This trio of a doctor, an insurance broker and an executive at a chemicals company were willing to make sacrifices to join the fight for democracy.

Like the student leaders, these more mature political activists shared much of the wider anger toward Hong Kong's cosseted elite. Many feel that the tycoons, who control much of the city's economy, have sold out their interests for a slice of Beijing's cash. I wanted to give the most privileged members of Generation HK a chance to tell their side of the story. Few were willing to talk to me at all, let alone grant an on-the-record interview.

Most of the offspring of the Hong Kong tycoons

remain a distant presence, disdainful of those who they fear want to destroy the world that has brought them immense riches. I could only find one man, Lau Ming-wai, the son of a billionaire fugitive from justice, who was willing to put his head above the parapet and engage with the real problems facing the city's youth, even if he had no easy answers.

While the business elite has never liked honest talk about politics, the city has had a thriving arts and cultural scene that feasted on Hong Kong's tensions and contradictions. A kind of West Berlin for China, it was home to writers, artists and film-makers who enjoyed freedoms that are unimaginable just across the border. As political divisions intensified over the last couple of years, Beijing and its supporters in Hong Kong cracked down on the arts sector. A few isolated acts of censorship can reverberate through a whole city, like the ripples fanning out from a pebble thrown into a pond.

I went to talk to some of the young artists who have seen their nascent success curtailed by this growing climate of control and self-censorship. Chief among them were the directors of *Ten Years*, a low-budget dystopian film about Hong Kong's future that was a surprise box-office hit, much to the disgust of the city's political and arts establishment. Not for long though, as it soon disappeared from cinemas without a trace. The pace of the erosion of Hong Kong's freedoms has inspired a more radical breed of young activists, who are pushing for independence and are willing to embrace violence as well as the ballot box.

When I first contacted the likes of Edward Leung and Chan Ho-tin, their political groups, Hong Kong Indigenous and the Hong Kong Nationalist Party, seemed so small as to be inconsequential. But, as the government carried out a series of cack-handed machinations to shut them up, support for their movements grew beyond all expectations, sending shockwaves to Beijing. Through a range of conversations with this diverse cast of young Hong Kongers, I hope to cast a spotlight on the generation that will set the future direction of a place that wants to remain 'Asia's world city'.

This is not a work of political science. The people I interviewed do not form a representative sample of Generation HK. Many of them, in fact, are among the city's most forthright voices. They do not speak for a generation so much as speak to it. From the activists to the artists and the rich kids to the would-be revolutionaries, they have all done things that have resonated with other young Hong Kongers through politics, education, movies or business. Amid these disparate voices, can we even define Generation HK and what drives them forward?

It is a common belief that identities are formed through exclusion, where a person can define oneself against the other.[1] For many young people today, being a Hong Konger means not being a Mainlander. Surveys show that fewer and fewer young Hong Kongers see themselves as 'Chinese'. A long-running poll by the respected public opinion programme at the University of Hong Kong shows that the proportion of residents who describe themselves as simply Chinese fell from a high of 39 per cent in 2008 to just 16 per cent by the end of 2016. Over the same period, the proportion who see themselves as a 'Hong Konger' or a 'Hong Konger in China' grew from 47 per cent to 64 per cent. Moreover, a survey by the Chinese University of Hong Kong found that nearly 40 per cent of those aged between 15 and 24 support the idea of independence from their neighbours in the Mainland.

To the extent that identities are defined against others, the simplest stereotypes pit free-thinking, considerate and flexible 'Hong Kongers' against a perception of 'Mainlanders' as dependent, greedy and eager to follow the party line. Of course, the reality is once again far more nuanced. Each person I interviewed had a different view on what it truly means to be a Hong Konger and some had little to say on the issue beyond the strong feeling that Hong Kong is their home. Identities are not formed around one centralised idea but are produced from a variety of concepts.[2] The question of Generation HK's identity does not just revolve around the idea of 'us' versus 'them'. Benedict Anderson, the late historian of Southeast Asia, developed a more positive understanding of nationalism by arguing that nations were formed because people start to see themselves as 'imagined communities' even though citizens may have drastically different life experiences.[3]

Despite the differences of opinion and background of those I interviewed, I was struck by just how many similarities there were in the Hong Kong that they imagined. Protecting the Cantonese language and the traditional Chinese writing system, defending the city's autonomy from Beijing and moving toward a more democratic future – these were aspirations that were shared by all. Clearly, in a short work such as this I can only scratch the surface of such a deep issue. Still, at a particularly acute moment in Hong Kong's history, it is important to ask these questions. I hope these discussions shed light on the spirit and determination of a generation fighting for their identity and freedom.

Ben Bland
Hong Kong
April 2017

I

The Student Leaders

At the height of the Occupy movement in 2014, when thousands of Hong Kongers shut down much of the city centre, images of student leader Joshua Wong were beamed around the world. With his bowl-cut hair, wiry frame and glasses, he was an unlikely figurehead for a street movement that was challenging one of the world's most powerful authoritarian states.

His nerdy, youthful appearance added to the allure for the international media. Journalists flocked to Hong Kong after the police used tear gas and pepper spray to try to disperse the demonstrators, prompting an outpouring of support from Hong Kongers and sympathisers around the world. *Time* magazine put him on its front cover, under the headline 'The Face of Protest'. Turning 18 years of age at the time, Wong told *Time*: 'I don't want to follow the games of adults, handing out business cards that you'll just put in the rubbish bin. [. . .] Political reform is not going to come from going to meetings.'

Just twenty months later, a rather different Wong turned up at the Foreign Correspondents Club in Hong Kong, a storied institution based in one of the few remaining colonial buildings in the main business district. There he gave a talk about his vision for Hong Kong and ditched his usual t-shirt and shorts for smart trousers, a white shirt and blue suit jacket. In his new guise as secretary general of a political party called Demosistō, he was merrily distributing the very business cards he had mocked previously.

He formed the party, whose name is a combination of the ancient Greek word for 'the people' and the Latin word for 'standing up', to contest elections for Hong Kong's partially democratic Legislative Council in September 2016. Forty of the seventy seats are elected by universal suffrage, while the rest are occupied by representatives of political, business and trade groups who mostly do the bidding of the Beijing government.

Standing in front of a lectern, Wong looked at home in front of the gathering of international journalists, business executives and diplomats. He told them he had felt 'depressed and downhearted' after the Umbrella Revolution failed in its objective of winning full democracy for Hong Kong. But, now, he and his friends were regaining their spirit after deciding to shift their battle for freedom and human rights into the field of electoral politics.

Wong himself was not able to stand for office, because there is a minimum age of twenty-one to enter LegCo – as the territory's council is known. Never easily dissuaded, he filed a judicial review to have the threshold lowered to the voting age of eighteen but failed. So Demosistō put forward 23-year-old Nathan Law, another student leader, as its candidate, with Wong and his friend Agnes Chow driving the campaign. Few established politicians or analysts gave them much chance of success. They questioned their maturity, noting wryly that many of their strongest supporters were not old enough to vote.

Trying to keep an open mind, I went to meet Nathan Law halfway through the campaign, on a blisteringly hot summer's day. He had just spent a sweaty morning accosting voters in Causeway Bay, where the narrow pavements channel huge crowds of Hong Kongers and Mainlanders into a dizzying array of shops selling everything from cut-price make-up to designer handbags.

Law had taken shelter in the air-conditioned confines of a funky co-working space owned by a friend. 'I'm definitely feeling tired,' he said as he greeted me with a weary handshake, less-than-enthused about the prospect of a two-hour grilling on his political views.

A cultural studies student at Hong Kong's Lingnan University, Law had climbed his way up the slippery ladder of varsity politics to become head of the Hong Kong Federation of Students. Now he was standing for election in Hong Kong island, a constituency full of bankers, accountants and the retired, their wealth matched only by their conservative attitudes. Winning their support was a much tougher challenge than corralling idealistic students.

'It's quite hard to deliver our message,' he said. 'A lot of people don't know what's happening in society and politics. Even those who are registered to vote might not care.' Under pressure from Beijing to squelch these young democrats, the powers-that-be were making life hard for Law and his Demosistō comrades.

The government's Companies Registry had refused to let the party establish a legal entity, rendering it impossible for them to open a bank account in which to receive donations. Although every candidate was entitled to a free mailshot, the authorities had censored Law's campaign leaflets because he had called for Hong Kong citizens to be given a referendum so that they could determine the territory's future status for themselves.

'Obviously, it's not a fair election,' he said, in between bites of a rice-cake and swigs of Yakult, the Japanese probiotic yoghurt drink, brought in by an aide who was trying to boost his energy levels. Law understood that the students' street campaigns had gone as far as they could. If they were serious about democratic reform and pushing back against China's encroachments in Hong Kong, they would need to broaden their appeal and find a more sustainable way to influence the political debate. While the Legislative Council was only partly democratic, it still had heft and a high profile in the eyes of many Hong Kongers. Law felt that putting the discussion of Hong Kong's future and the question of sovereignty on the table in the council chamber would have far more impact than nattering away at a roadside stall or on a radio talk show.

Despite his downbeat manner, Law was clearly driven by a sense of mission. Alongside Wong and Chow, he wanted to build a social movement that could grow from the streets to the centre of power, inspiring others by their example. That would be a rare feat indeed. Other Occupy demonstrations from Wall Street to London had been dominated by the usual suspects and had failed to expand their base beyond small groups of anti-capitalists, animal rights campaigners and lifestyle protesters. In Hong Kong, there was much more at stake.

With their culture under threat from China, their economic opportunities limited and no hinterland in which to flee, many youngsters had little hope in the future. 'Young people can't afford to buy a property, their salaries are lower than ten years ago and the wealth gap is the largest among all advanced countries and regions,'

Law explained.

All around us in Causeway Bay, people were spending obscene amounts of money on luxury goods, allowing the store operators to cover some of the most expensive retail rents in the world. This highly conspicuous consumption by the few obscured the financial struggles of the many. Superficially prosperous, Hong Kong is much more troubled underneath the surface, like a polished apple rotting from within. The territory's fanciest flats high up on the Peak on Hong Kong island cost tens of millions of dollars each. A single car parking space at one such apartment block sold for US$620 000 in 2016, more than the cost of most Hong Kongers' homes.

These luxury flats afford towering views over the harbour and the ageing high-rise apartment buildings that line many of the city's roads. But they are too far away to peek inside these blocks and see the cramped conditions with which most Hong Kongers are forced to cope. Soaring property prices have benefited the wealthy at the cost of everyone else.

Some 200 000 Hong Kongers can only afford to live in tiny sub-divided homes, which are made out of flats and industrial units partitioned into miserable quarters with a median area of just 10 square metres. The median monthly rent for these cubicles in 2015 was HK$4200 or US$540, according to a survey by the government. Thousands of the poorest Hong Kongers live in 'cage homes', bunk beds enmeshed in wire like rabbit hutches. When bow-tie-wearing former Hong Kong leader Donald Tsang was jailed in February 2017 for misconduct in public office, some joked that at least his cell would be bigger than many subdivided homes and come rent-free. Squeezed financially and spatially, yet without any means to effect meaningful political change, it is all too easy for Hong Kong's citizens to despair.

Amid the gloom, Law was trying to promote a brighter message. 'Even though you're disappointed about the current situation, you still have to store hope in your heart and try to do something,' he said.

Law's journey to a frontline soldier in the battle against the Chinese Communist party was unlikely, but it said much about the generational changes roiling Hong Kong. Born in Mainland China, he spent his first six years in the sprawling metropolis of Shenzhen, just across the border from Hong Kong. He only moved to the former British colony in 1999, two years after it was handed back to Beijing's control. His parents were blue-collar workers, with no interest in politics, like many who had learnt to steer clear of trouble in the Mainland. In Hong Kong, they settled in Tung Chung, one of many new towns built to cater to a population that expanded rapidly from the 1950s to the present day, thanks to immigration from across the border. Law attended a pro-establishment school that he said was 'funded by red money' – meaning that its backers were promoting the territory's further integration into China. The trigger for his conversion from loyalist to rebel came in 2010, when Chinese dissident writer Liu Xiaobo was given the Nobel Peace Prize in recognition of his long struggle to promote human rights.

The award infuriated Beijing. The Chinese government turned its ire on normally inoffensive Norway, whose parliamentarians appoint the committee that chooses the winner, downgrading diplomatic relations and initiating a boycott of Norwegian salmon. The headmaster of Law's school followed the party line, using an assembly the day after the award to lambast Liu as a puppet controlled by 'foreign forces'. Something about this theatrical denunciation jarred with the young Law. 'Those who receive that award should be great people,' he said. 'So I started wondering what's happening in my school?'

In dozens of conversations with establishment businesspeople and politicians who expressed their love for China, I was told that young democrats in Hong Kong were mollycoddled, ignorant brats. They only rebelled against the system – so it was claimed – because they knew nothing about China and the merits of its transformation from poverty-stricken backwater to economic giant. Law had spent more time in the Mainland than many of these self-professed patriots, who enjoy the profits they make in China but prefer to live in Hong Kong with its uncensored internet, high standards of food safety and rigorous legal system. He insisted that these tycoons and government officials had it the wrong way around.

'A lot of people think we don't know China, so we hate them,' he said. 'Actually, we know China, so that's why we hate them.' He spat out these words not with venom but with a sense of exasperation. Battling authoritarianism is a lonely struggle.

Over eight years reporting in Asia, from Singapore to China and Myanmar to Vietnam, I had seen how repressive governments and their secret police forces grind down activists like Law. Their tactics work so well not just because of the physical limits they place on people but because of the psychological impact, which strains friendships and family ties. While many others would be deterred, Law was pushing back against the repression he saw coming from the Mainland.

In addition to the problems he had faced during Occupy and then the election, Law's family members in the Mainland had been visited by the police and pressured to get him to cease his activism. He said that no such threats would stop him, whatever the consequences. His resolve was impressive. Yet, his sombre tone left me doubting whether he thought he could really get elected. He was clearly better at convincing

Hong Kong's voters than me.

On 5 September, as the count was concluded the day after a record turnout, Law made history when he became the youngest-ever person elected to the Legislative Council. He had won 50 818 votes, the second highest total of the six legislators returned on Hong Kong island, after Regina Ip, one of the city's best-known pro-Beijing politicians. Several weeks later, I went to Hong Kong Baptist University to discuss the result with Agnes Chow, the youngest and most cheerful of the Demosistō triumvirate.

*

Wearing a t-shirt emblazoned with the slogan 'from the masses', the 19-year-old was eating a chocolate brownie as I approached her at the main café on campus. 'I'm full of energy,' she said with an endearing smile, having just finished a table-tennis class. Physical education is compulsory at her university, where she is studying the theory of politics while spending much of her time on the real thing. Chow was surprised by the election result, never imagining that Demosistō could win, and by such a large margin, because of their lack of experience.

With twenty days to go until the election, it was not looking good. The young politicians feared a big defeat that would be a heavy blow to the democracy movement in Hong Kong – and provide ballast to those who argued that these naïve students could not reach out beyond their peer group. No wonder Nathan Law had seemed downbeat. Regardless of speculation, they decided to make one last push, extending their street campaigning until midnight in Causeway Bay to catch shoppers and restaurant goers as they went home on the many buses that criss-cross the district.

Having got over the line, they are now feeling a different kind of pressure, fearing they will disappoint the tens of thousands of voters who put their faith in Demosistō. And despite her sunny manner, and cherubic looks, the diminutive Agnes Chow knows all about pressure.

Around the same time that Wong was slapped on the front cover of *Time,* Agnes Chow suddenly quit the Occupy protests, saying the movement had worn her out 'physically and psychologically'. Later, she told me that her family had been leant on to make her give up the fight. Even now she declined to say who threatened them and how, for fear of jeopardising their safety further. But she struck a defiant tone.

'I'll not again make a decision that the central government wants to see,' she said. 'For me and the people around me, we learnt a great lesson after that kind of experience. [. . .] When we faced violence from the police and suppression from the authorities, it made me braver and gave me more courage to fight against the regime.'

The hard-line approach taken by Beijing and its allies in Hong Kong toward these young activists keeps backfiring. Nathan Law was turned by heavy-handed Communist propaganda from his headmaster. Joshua Wong and Agnes Chow were politicised by the Hong Kong government's attempt to implement a school programme designed to breed a generation of Chinese patriots, known as Moral and National Education. Such efforts to inculcate a sense of Chinese identity are prompting these young Hong Kongers to think more deeply about who they are and what they stand for. But not in the way intended. Rather, they are imagining a Hong Kong defined by the struggle for political freedom and democracy.

In 2011, when Joshua Wong was just fifteen and more fond of computer games than politics, he founded a group called Scholarism to fight against what he – and many Hong Kongers – saw as Communist brainwashing. Spreading through secondary schools, the backlash culminated in a huge protest of more than 100 000 people outside the main government offices in 2012. The authorities eventually relented, dropping the proposals for patriotic education. It was a major victory for Wong and his friends, which convinced them that they could push for more.

Until Agnes Chow read about Wong and Scholarism on Facebook in 2012, she too, had been more interested in Japanese cartoons than education policy. 'I was really surprised and impressed because I never thought youngsters the same age as me could do such mature acts against the government,' she said. 'I admired those kinds of actions and wanted to be one of them.'

Chow, Wong and Law are routinely derided by the Chinese government and its acolytes in Hong Kong as idealistic fools, troublemakers and tools of 'hostile foreign forces' who want to destroy the Chinese nation. But they have succeeded in going from the streets to the legislature precisely because many Hong Kongers do take them seriously and admire their willingness to fight for a better city.

Now, they are trying to mature as a political force, extending their organisation's reach beyond their couple of hundred volunteers. With ample funding from the Legislative Council, they plan to set up district offices around Hong Kong island and build support from the ground up by tackling more everyday issues such as the shortage of affordable housing. 'The core problem of Hong Kong is not only politics and sovereignty but also lifestyle and whether we have autonomy in our own lives,' Chow said.

*

Joshua Wong certainly does not lack any autonomy, as

he flies around the world trying to generate support for the fight for democracy and an eventual referendum on Hong Kong's future status.

In November 2016, he went to Washington D.C. to meet leading members of the US Congress, including Nancy Pelosi, the Minority Leader of the House of Representatives, and Marco Rubio, the ambitious Republican Senator and former presidential candidate. The young Hong Kong politician even donned a tie, grinning like a schoolboy in posed photos with the powerbrokers of Capitol Hill that he uploaded to his Facebook and Twitter feeds. Beijing, predictably, was not happy. The Chinese Foreign Ministry warned that 'those who try to buoy themselves up by leaning onto foreign forces' can expect that their schemes 'will come to no avail'.[4]

Alex Lo, a cranky columnist at the *South China Morning Post*, Hong Kong's main English-language daily newspaper, was not very impressed either. In a piece entitled 'Watch out for Joshua Wong's new-found friends in Washington', he warned that democracy campaigners in Hong Kong would try to play to the anti-China tendencies of the recently elected US President Donald Trump and the Republican-controlled Congress.[5] Lo called them dupes who were 'happy to attach strings to themselves for the Americans to pull'.

Catching up with Joshua Wong a few weeks before

his US trip, it was clear to me that he was anything but a puppet. There is no denying that he enjoys being fêted by esteemed bodies from the US Congress to the Oxford Union, the British university's debating society. He also had a worrying tendency to refer to himself in the third person, a verbal tic of grandiose leaders from Julius Caesar to Donald Trump and a signal of his own political ambitions.

'Building a party is a goal for me to prove to people in Hong Kong and even in the world that, if in the previous four years, Joshua Wong was a student leader, in the next four years Joshua Wong is not just a student leader,' he told me as we grabbed a late Sunday lunch in Minh & Kok, a fashionable Vietnamese-Thai restaurant.

Pinning down a meeting with these young activists is never easy. They do not tend to answer their mobile phones, preferring to use WhatsApp, Telegram or other messaging apps. Even then they respond only sporadically and have a rather fluid approach toward arrangements. Wong had moved our meeting five or six times before I eventually nailed him down. To be fair, he was in the middle of some serious problems.

Just days before, he had been in court – alongside Nathan Law and another student activist – where the government was appealing to have them jailed following an earlier conviction for unlawful assembly. Luckily for them, the appeal court upheld the previous decision to give them only community service or suspended jail terms for breaking into the forecourt of the government offices in September 2014, an act that kick-started the Occupy protests. At the same time, Wong was planning a trip to Bangkok to talk to Thai students, while expecting that the Chinese government would nudge Thailand's military junta to deny him entry, as Malaysia had done previously. He was subsequently detained on arrival and deported.

So I felt somewhat sympathetic as Wong kept interrupting our conversation to check the cascade of messages on his phone. The relentless texting was straining the battery and, as it ran out of juice, I offered him my power-bank. I wondered if I was becoming one of the 'hostile foreign forces' assisting China's enemies. For I was not only powering but also feeding the revolution.

Lunch was on me and after wolfing down a bowl of noodle soup with slurpy abandon, Wong swiftly ordered some spring rolls to satisfy his remaining hunger. 'This is a good restaurant,' he said as he wiped his mouth with a tissue. 'The price is not expensive and it's quiet. Otherwise people will say "Hey you're Joshua Wong, just take a photo". It's quite annoying sometimes.'

Fittingly, some minutes later, a young, wealthy-looking Hong Kong couple came up to our table and the woman tapped him on the shoulder. Speaking in English, she said: 'Sorry to interrupt but we just want to tell you that you're doing a great job and we're all very proud of you.' Despite his earlier moan about selfie fatigue, he looked humbled and thanked the couple profusely before rolling another spring roll in lettuce, dipping it in fish sauce and taking a big bite.

In addition to the praise, Wong has received his fair share of abuse, from knuckle-dragging regime loyalists to the radical student leaders who prefer burning Chinese flags and fighting the police to peaceful civil disobedience. I wondered what drives him to keep going. It is not a simple story.

His father is a small businessman and his mother is a family counsellor. Wong grew up in a middle-class housing estate on Ap Lei Chau. Connected to Hong Kong island by bridge, it is the second most densely populated isle in the world but a pleasant place to live, with beautiful views over the South China Sea. Many of his supporters come from similarly comfortable origins.

Observers could tell that the main Occupy site near the government offices in Admiralty was full of people with middle-class backgrounds, he said, 'because everything was quite clean, students had to study and there was a lot of art and music'. Some radical protesters found this revolt of the nerds laughable but Wong defended this uniquely Hong Kong movement, where people resisted the police by day and swotted up on their mathematics at night. 'You have to respect the truth that these people who engage in civil disobedience still feel they need a study centre to do their homework,' he said. Not to appear *too* uncool, he added with a smirk that he 'in fact did *not* do homework during the Umbrella movement.'

Like so many others I met in Hong Kong, Wong was swept into the world of political activism by opposition to Chinese encroachment into their lives. This attitude was inextricably linked to a questioning of their identity, as well as their political campaigns for democracy.

'In the past, we said that we do not love the Communist party but we still love the country and we are part of China,' he explained. 'Now we just say we are ethnically Chinese but not people in China. [. . .] While the country does not allow me to enter, so how can I love it?' he added, in reference to the fact that he, Law and many other activists have been banned from entering the Mainland. Not being part of Mainland China is the first element of this burgeoning Hong Kong identity.

Still, being from Mainland China is not a problem in itself because the core of the Hong Kong identity was about values, not genes or place of birth, as Wong told me. 'I hope every Hong Konger can agree on democracy, human rights, freedom, rule of law and the separation of powers,' he said. This idealistic stance stood in stark contrast to the more xenophobic conceptions of Hong Kong identity that I would soon discover more about.

In the past, Wong has said that his Christian religion pushed him to think about these values and have the courage to fight for his beliefs. Unlike the American politicians who are accused of pulling his strings, he does not want to labour the point. He sees his religion as an issue of personal conscience rather than a tool with which to reach out to other young people yearning for answers at a time of trouble. 'Christianity motivates me to care about politics and society,' he said. 'But I'm not saying that I'm pushing for self-determination because God or Jesus gave me a signal. I don't want religion to become the instrument for me to gain some support or social capital.'

Wong likes to say that by overturning the patriotic education plan, then organising the massive Occupy protests and now securing electoral success, young Hong Kongers have 'turned something impossible to possible'. However, even many of those who are sympathetic to Demosistō feel that their next goal – to secure a legally-binding referendum on Hong Kong's future – is genuinely impossible.

For Xi Jinping and China's other Communist leaders, acknowledging the right of Hong Kongers to determine their own future is tantamount to accepting that China has no right to sovereignty over the territory. To them, campaigning for self-determination is as dangerous an act of splittism as calling for independence.

Wong admits that much depends on the future trajectory of Communist rule in China, something which Western experts have been terrible at predicting. The chances of winning international support for his referendum plan anytime soon look minuscule, given most countries' eagerness for more trade and investment with China and their reluctance to upset Beijing unnecessarily. Still, from Mahatma Gandhi, the Indian independence leader, to Nigel Farage, the British campaigner against the European Union, no activist ever got what they wanted by worrying too much about what is practicable. 'I was born in Hong Kong, I live in Hong Kong, I love Hong Kong and I hope Hong Kong has a better future,' said Wong. 'We want to determine our destiny.'

All three of the Demosistō trio had been driven into politics while at school, coming face-to-face with institutions heavily influenced by China's ideology, and they all spoke of their frustrations with and fears for Hong Kong's educational system. Agnes Chow, in particular, in-between her studies and politics, still found time to teach English to a group of high-school pupils. Like many in Hong Kong, these pupils had turned to an extra tutor to help them pass the tough exams that define life chances in this cut-throat city. It is, she said, a 'horrible' system where some primary school pupils are sent to tutorial classes seven days a week and parents take their toddlers to interview classes so they can get into the best kindergartens.

The school system in Hong Kong defied many of the principles of modern liberal education. After class, instead of broadening their horizons or overcoming their personal shortcomings, students here were going to organised 'cram' schools for hours of extra rote learning. Exam success is so important in Hong Kong that the tutors who could unlock the secrets to getting high marks could attract big followings and big money. But, in a brutally competitive industry, these super-tutors were under almost as much pressure as their stressed-out pupils.

II

The Super Tutors

Lawsuits, multimillion-dollar talent wars and die-hard fans. The world of Hong Kong's infamous tutors was a bizarre one indeed. As I struggled to make sense of it, I decided to approach the best-known and best-paid tutor of them all: Lam Yat-yan.

When I met Lam, he had gone to ground, and with good reason. Hong Kong's press pack was after him and when they get the bit between their teeth, they can rival even the most hound-like of tabloid journalists. Lam had all the trappings of any other celebrity, in a city that worships money and success: flash sports cars, legions of young devotees and his picture plastered on billboards all over town. Reporters were desperate to get to him because he was at the centre of a very public battle for his talent.

A rival organisation had taken out advertisements in

several Hong Kong newspapers, offering the 28-year-old a HK$85 million – or US$11 million – annual pay packet if he agreed to join them. In any other place in the world, this would be a story about a rising football star or the latest hot young singer to go viral on social media. In Hong Kong, such tales of internecine competition point to something seemingly more prosaic: exam cramming schools.

In an industry where the best teachers can earn millions of dollars, YY Lam, as he is known, is the undoubted king of the tutors. High-school students flock to his Chinese language classes every year seeking inspiration and crucial tips on how to pass the Hong Kong Diploma of Secondary Education. The Chinese HKDSE exam is the toughest test in one of the world's most brutally competitive education systems. Students call it the 'paper of death' because it is so difficult, and a poor mark can easily undermine their chances of getting a university place, even if they perform well in other papers such as English and Maths. I wanted to understand how after-school tutors could become millionaires and what the existence of this strange business revealed about the pressures facing young people.

Lam was the perfect person to help me make sense of it but he was also extremely wary. It took months to convince him and his cohort of aides – who he calls 'YY's team' – to talk to me. His office was located on the thirteenth floor of a narrow office building in the crowded commercial district of Mong Kok. This is the Hong Kong of movie scenes, with taxis and minibuses clogging streets that are lined with shoppers, traders and delivery men, overhung by outsized neon signs advertising restaurants and karaoke bars.

A few days after our meeting, Mong Kok was turned into a war zone of equally filmic proportions. A government crackdown on protests in defence of unlicensed street hawkers morphed into a rolling all-night riot dubbed the 'Fishball Revolution', with cars set alight and police firing warning shots into the air. But all was calm as I shook hands with Lam and entered his small office on a sunny yet crisp February morning. On first impression, he looked every bit the vapid celebrity, with his expertly-coiffed hair, tight-fitting clothes and air of self-importance. Once we started to talk, it became clear that underneath the K-pop image was a thoughtful, conscientious and somewhat nervous individual.

'I was surprised and shocked,' he said of the brazen attempt by Modern Education, a rival tutoring company, to poach him from his current school, Beacon College. He was still reluctant to talk about the details. 'Please don't make this the focus,' he said. 'Because we are working in education, money is not something that we want to discuss too much.' Luckily for me, Beacon had revealed its key financial information in a public

38

prospectus in 2015, when it was planning to float on the stock exchange in Hong Kong.

The company, which is one of Hong Kong's biggest cramming schools, said that its top tutor was paid HK$35 million in the previous financial year and that he was responsible for generating 40 per cent of its annual revenue of HK$328 million.[6] Was that star tutor Lam, as widely suspected? He tried, half-heartedly, to brush off the question. 'I can't confirm,' he said. 'But it's obvious.'

Born to working-class parents, Lam never imagined that he could amass such a fortune, nor that teaching Chinese could be his route to riches. His father made clothes' labels in a factory before the business joined most of Hong Kong's other manufacturers, moving to Mainland China in search of cheaper wages. His mother worked – and still does – in a bakery. Lam's accession to the tutor-king throne began by chance, with an incident that he said foretold the stresses faced by teachers and pupils alike in Hong Kong.

One of Beacon's young, hard-working Chinese tutors had died suddenly after a class, amid suggestions that he had been suffering from overwork, Lam said. The school asked the professors at the Chinese University of Hong Kong to refer a possible replacement and they suggested Lam, a graduate Chinese student at the time. 'I just wanted to give it a try as I was young,' he said.

Lam had read the stories of wealthy super-tutors in the media. But he knew that most tutors had unspectacular careers and struggled to make ends meet. By the end of his first year, however, he realised he had made a good decision as he watched his student numbers rise rapidly. They were attracted by his enthusiasm, understanding of how to tackle university entrance exams and his image as 'cool and successful at the same time'.

Today, Lam has more than 10 000 students, most of them attending live video broadcasts of classes. He had to cut back on teaching in person as he was swamped with questions from enraptured pupils.

*

The super tutor's path to wealth is supported by the constraints placed on young people in Hong Kong from their peers, parents and society. Across East Asia, mothers and fathers instil in their offspring a Darwinian approach to educational and professional competition. In Hong Kong, weighty expectations are compounded by extreme competition, for school and university places, good jobs and decent housing. Generation HK is being moulded by these forces, for worse and for better.

Only around 20 per cent of school leavers get into one of the eight publicly-funded universities, according to government data. From this choke point, the pressure is squeezed up, and down. Unless you have graduated from one of these universities – or your parents are wealthy enough to send you overseas – you will struggle to find well-paying employment and will never be able to afford even the tiniest of bolt-hole apartments. Therefore, many high-school students in Hong Kong take extra tuition in order to boost their scores in the HKDSE and their chance of getting a university place. Their parents also fight to get them into the best high school, which means extra tuition at primary school. To be accepted into a quality primary school, it also helps if your kids have had interview training. And so on, down to even the level of kindergarten.

Many young Hong Kongers told me that immigration from Mainland China has added to the educational strains upon them. It is not just a question of increased competition in quantitative terms. Several students said that they worried that their Mainland peers were better schooled, more hard-working and more adept at technical subjects, in particular. Some even admitted that during freshers' week at university they would deliberately avoid signing up for classes with too many Mainland students for fear that they would be pushed too far down the exam rankings. It was part of an inferiority-superiority complex that many young Hong Kongers had toward China.

On the one hand, many historically saw their

Mainland cousins as poor, badly educated and narrow-minded. On the other, the rise of China over the last few decades means that the Chinese middle class is now much bigger, better educated and more well-travelled. So while many still look down on Mainlanders, they also fear competing with them. This tension is at the heart of Generation HK's struggle to define who they really are.

*

The first time I saw Billy Ng was on a bus. Then I kept coming across him in train stations. Posters advertising 'Billy Ng and his Elite English Team' seemed to be everywhere, his face staring intently at passers-by and promising to help improve their English scores in university entrance exams. Naturally, I was excited when I finally managed to persuade Beacon, which shared his services with another tuition company called King's Glory, to let me sit in on one of his classes. Intrigued but still baffled by the scale of the business, I wanted to experience some of this madness for myself.

One Sunday evening, late in the summer, I made the long journey by Hong Kong's efficient metro system to Tuen Mun. A suburban new town in the far north-west of the New Territories, it is far closer to Shenzhen, the neighbouring Mainland mega-city, than it is to Hong Kong island. As the train shuttled between the long stops, the sun was starting to set over the steep, verdant hills in the distance. It felt less intense than other parts of Hong Kong, where the skyscrapers, apartment buildings, pedestrians and vehicles fought for every square inch of space. But as I arrived at the small mall where Beacon holds its classes in Tuen Mun, it was clear that the pressure on students here was no different.

Outside each classroom, teenage students were lined up neatly against the wall. In most countries, kids fight it out for the seats at the back of the class, as far from the teacher's gaze as possible. At Beacon however, they take queuing numbers to prevent any jostling for the desks right in front of the tutor. An officious, pint-sized guard from G4S – the ubiquitous global security company that I encountered everywhere from Hong Kong to Papua New Guinea – was patrolling the corridors to keep order. She even stopped the Beacon executive escorting me to ask why we were not in the queue, after mistaking us for students.

My feeling that the kids were not here for the love of learning only deepened as I entered the classroom after all the students had taken their assigned seats. Bright strip lighting illuminated the small room, where thirty tiny desks were squeezed in, barely an elbow's breadth apart. It was windowless, except for one glass panel down the left-hand-side that looked on to an adjoining class of thirty. This was a way to get around Hong Kong government regulations that limit class sizes in tutorial centres, one of several measures designed to rein in the worst excesses of this sometimes rapacious industry.

A sign on the wall featuring a pair of handcuffs warned students that they could face prosecution for theft of intellectual property if they filmed the lesson. I had hoped that by coming to an English class run by one of Hong Kong's most famous English tutors, I would be able to understand much of the proceedings, but I was sorely mistaken. From the moment Ng plugged in his microphone, turned up the volume to an ear-achingly unpleasant level and started barking away, all instruction was in Cantonese. He spoke non-stop for 90 minutes, taking no questions during the class and asking the students none. It was the sort of studying that would give liberal education gurus a fit.

I was struggling to stay awake but the students were hanging on to his every word and not just because their parents had stumped up HK$125 for each lesson. They believe Ng – and other top tutors – can give them the model answers they need to pass their exams. 'When it comes to', 'second to none', 'no room for complacency' – these tick-generating phrases were the only English words that came out of Ng's mouth. Each time he uttered one and highlighted it on the projector at the front of the class, every student carefully marked it down in their textbook using exactly the same combination of biro ink and coloured pens as Ng. Once the humourless drilling was finally over, past 8 p.m., Ng sat down to talk to me.

Having taught five such sessions that day, he was knackered. Still, dressed in an Abercrombie & Fitch t-shirt, blue jeans and shiny Adidas trainers, he looked every bit his twenty-four years of age. YY Lam's entry into this weird world was facilitated by the unexpected death of a predecessor. Ng also owes his successful life as a tutor to misfortune, albeit his own.

'Originally I wanted to be a lawyer but the admissions requirements were too strict so I studied for a bachelor of business administration degree,' he said. 'I never thought I would become a teacher.' He started teaching English classes part-time to earn some cash while at university and found that he had a talent for attracting students and, perhaps more importantly, predicting future exam questions. 'I have to spend a lot of time analysing exam trends,' he said, with a sigh. 'This job has become my life.'

When not reading through past exam papers, he is answering student queries on Facebook or preparing for classes. 'I basically have no holiday,' he said. 'I need to prove my value to the students by helping them get good results.'

Does he worry that the tutoring industry is simply adding to the burdens weighing down young people while teaching them little? Not at all. 'The job of school teachers is to impart knowledge,' he explained. 'The tutor's responsibility is to help students get into university. Young people just have to get over the pressure. That's life.'

Despite their successful careers, Ng and Lam feel the competitive heat just as much as their students. Tutors typically work as contractors for businesses such as Beacon or its main rivals, Modern Education and King's Glory. They earn most of their money through revenue-sharing agreements based on how many students they teach. But this is a dying industry, literally. As Hong Kong's population ages because of a low birth rate, the number of high-school students is falling rapidly.

Hong Kong has more than 900 tuition centres focused on high-school pupils but enrolments dropped from more than 200 000 in 2010 to 180 000 in 2014, according to a report commissioned by Beacon and produced by Euromonitor, the market research group.[7] With the pool of possible customers shrinking, the tutorial centres have been engaged in a bitter war for tutors and students.

Regulations add to the tensions. The government prevents schools from collecting annual fees in order to stop them ripping off parents. So the schools and tutors have to work very hard to stop students leaving. 'The competition is cut-throat and it's not easy to keep the quality of the lessons,' admitted Ng.

Multimillionaire YY Lam may drive a US$190 000

sports car and enjoy a revered status among young people in Hong Kong but he seems just as nervous about his future prospects. To stay on top of his game, he has a support team of more than a hundred full- and part-time staff. Like Ng, he rarely takes leave and even has a bed in his office for the days when preparatory work overwhelms him. 'Even now, I am still jittery,' he said. 'In this industry, if you make one mistake, or your passion fades, the students would feel it. There will be an instant drop. That's why I said it's a high-pressure business.'

*

To better understand the strains of Hong Kong's education system, I arranged to meet two young students who attended classes by YY Lam and other famous tutors. Tiffany Lai and Richard Kwok are both smart, ambitious and confident, with an irrepressible enthusiasm to make Hong Kong a better place. Yet they both fell foul of the HKDSE exams. Neither got the grades necessary to go straight to university. So they are studying for an associate degree in social work, which may allow them to transfer to a full degree course later.

'Hong Kong is a stressful place, and it all starts at kindergarten,' Lai told me over a coffee in Causeway Bay. 'The question many parents ask themselves is: do you want your kid to be a loser or a winner?'

Lai, who is 18 years old, decided several years ago that she did not want to go down the conventional path. Marrying her love of theatre with her desire to promote social change, she wanted to become a drama therapist, using role-playing and theatre to help troubled young people work through their problems. But, to win a place at university she still had to pass the dreaded Chinese school-leaving exam. So she signed up for YY Lam's classes.

'Lam says that you can change your marks over just one summer in the sixth form, which is the key moment to determine your life,' said Lai. 'Besides his teaching method, the way he encourages students is very impressive. Some people even cry in his class when he tells the story [that] he was not a very good student at secondary school.'

Some tutors sell themselves based purely on their ability to coach exam-boosting techniques, while others pitch themselves more as inspirational figures. Lam combines both traits. 'He gives us a lot of support and exam tips that we could not get from our school teachers,' said 19-year-old Richard Kwok. But while they have benefited from the tutorial centres, these students also have serious qualms about the industry and its values.

Lai recently took a part-time job teaching primary school pupils at a tutorial centre but quit after just a few months. 'It was very stressful and the teaching was not very meaningful,' she said. 'We had to look through so many past exam papers to prepare and then walk around a class shouting at kids through a microphone to push them to work faster.'

Around the world, every school system struggles to find the right balance between broad learning and exam preparation. The unique dynamics of Hong Kong have resulted in a counter-productive situation where education is turned into an existential fight that neither fosters real talent nor does much to help the average kid. Lam, Ng and other star tutors have used their skills and nous to capitalise on this weakness, epitomising the freewheeling entrepreneurial spirit of Hong Kong. Sadly, they themselves have become stuck in a similar cycle of intense competition and stress. While their students look up to them as role models, they embody the long-term problems with Hong Kong's education system as well as offering short-term solutions.

The issues facing education in Hong Kong encapsulate the wider tension between the city's Western and Chinese values. There is a strong desire from the likes of Lai, Kwok and many others to see the city move toward a more Westernised school system, where broad-based learning is valued over test results alone. That is coming up against the strong Chinese tradition that puts exam performance over all else.

Facing such heavy pressures in school and university,

many of those who make it professionally keep their heads down and stay out of politics, focusing on getting promotions and pay rises. Activists bemoan the dominance of these 'Hong Kong pigs' who they accuse of doing nothing for society. However, a small but growing band are starting to challenge this perception. As they push back against the constraints of adult life and societal expectations, they are unleashing their passion for change.

III

The Professional Democrats

Hong Kong's educational conveyor belt is meant to produce accountants, bankers and lawyers who will keep the economy ticking over in a city that is reliant on financial services and trade with China. Their mission, as the political establishment would have it, is to make money, keep their mouths shut when it comes to sensitive issues and produce another generation of besuited drones. So something must have gone terribly wrong with Kelvin Lee.

An ambitious insurance broker in his early twenties, he used to care more about selling policies than meddling in politics. Yet, everything changed on 28 September 2014, when he decided to take a look at the early stages of the Occupy protest near the main government offices in Hong Kong. As the police grew alarmed by the growing numbers gathering for what they regarded as an illegal assembly, they fired tear gas and charged with batons raised in an attempt to disperse the crowd. 'That day was really remarkable for me,' said Lee, now twenty-six. 'I saw the tear gas explode in front of me more than twenty times and saw how frightened people were.'

At that time, he did not agree with the protesters' demands for democratic reforms but felt the urge to defend the students from the police assault. Roused by the Occupy spirit, he started to wonder what he could do himself to promote a better future for Hong Kong. For the first time in his life, he started to read about Hong Kong's strange political system, determined to learn before he could plot a way to change it from the inside.

Fresh-faced and wearing an expertly ironed white shirt, Lee came straight from work to meet me at the upscale mall in the International Financial Centre development on the central waterfront. Talking in a deliberate and earnest fashion, he explained his metamorphosis from unquestioning finance worker to a disciple of political change.

'There are about 100 000 people working in insurance but no-one talks about politics in the office, not even during the Umbrella revolution,' he said. 'Are these people living in Hong Kong or what? They are just working and living as normal, as if nothing happened.' During the seventy-nine days that central Hong Kong was occupied, Lee met several other people from his industry on the streets and together they decided to do something, forming a pro-democracy lobby group called Insurance Arise. It is very small, with just ten to fifteen members, and it is one of several similar organisations founded in recent years by professionals trying to extend the fight for freedom and Hong Kong's values to a broader audience. Action Accountants, IT Voice and Financier Conscience: the very names of these groups are designed to belie the stereotypes about professionals in Hong Kong (and beyond).

Like Insurance Arise, these groups have struggled to attract members and to convince them to speak out publicly. But, it seemed to me that the attitudes of the professionals I met on a regular basis through my work for the *Financial Times* were starting to change. That was because Hong Kong's freedoms and way of life were coming under greater strain. Many were shaken by the kidnapping of five booksellers by Chinese security agents in 2015, a blatant and damaging breach of Hong Kong's autonomy. More generally, the Chinese government was playing an ever greater role in Hong Kong politics, the media and daily life through the machinations of its secretive Liaison Office, which is housed in a sinister-looking building in a western suburb of Hong Kong island.

One friend in his late twenties who works for an international investment bank told me that he had been 'pissed off' with the protesters during Occupy because they had not only interrupted his commute but damaged Hong Kong's reputation for political stability. Now my friend had come to the realisation that he needed Joshua Wong and the rest to fight on his behalf. 'People like me are not willing to speak out because we might get sacked,' he said. 'So we need these guys to defend our rights as China tries to take them away.'

Kelvin Lee has become one of those guys. He stepped up because no-one else was willing to. The youngest member of Insurance Arise, he is also the spokesperson. The way he sees it, he has much less to sacrifice, career-wise, than more senior colleagues with bigger salaries and families to support. Despite what he said, he was taking substantial risks.

Much of Hong Kong's insurance business – and the broader financial services industry – is set up to serve clients from Mainland China. Many of the customers are wealthy individuals who buy Hong Kong insurance policies as a way to get their money out of China, bypassing the government's capital controls, which restrict large transfers of cash. Lee's current employer is not only Mainland focused, it is a Mainland company. His experience working there demonstrated to him just how deeply Beijing was encroaching into Hong Kong's affairs.

One week before the Legislative Council polls,

when Nathan Law was elected, Lee's boss called a company-wide meeting. She told the assembled staff that they should vote for someone who would 'do the right thing' for Hong Kong, not those who were 'breaking the law and breaking everything'. As if that message, straight from the Communist officials working at the Liaison Office, was not clear enough, she offered the insurance brokers a list of which pro-government candidates to vote for. 'Many of my colleagues wanted the list because they really didn't know who the nominees are,' Lee told me. He found such unsubtle meddling laughable but knew it was pretty effective, especially as it was repeated across Hong Kong at many companies with Mainland ownership or close Mainland ties. Some professionals are scared they will damage their career prospects if they go against their bosses' orders. Others simply do not care about anything other than making money, maintaining their lifestyle and supporting their family. Either way, it was and is extremely tough for the likes of Lee to convince his colleagues that it is worth fighting for his vision of Hong Kong's future.

In 2015, he and his comrades at Insurance Arise started collecting signatures for a petition to reform the voting system in Hong Kong. Insurance is one of the several so-called functional constituencies that are given thirty of the seventy seats in the Legislative Council. Some industries have open, democratic votes for their legislative representatives. The insurance seat is also subject to a vote, in theory, but all the voters are corporations, many of them foreign groups like AXA, HSBC and Prudential. Lee was campaigning for partial democratic reforms that would give each insurance worker a vote in their own industry constituency. Even then, Insurance Arise was only able to collect 1000 signatures despite spending three months at street stands outside the main insurance company headquarters.

'We weren't asking people to commit, just to listen. But no-one would stay for more than two minutes. You know Hong Kong people, always rushing,' he said. 'Through this year we kept thinking, Should we continue this because there are not many results here?'

What then, I wondered, did keep him going? Despite the growing problems, Lee said he does not want to leave a city he loves. So he has no choice but to fight for a better future. The urgency of his struggle is growing day by day, as he watches Hong Kong's autonomy slipping away. Politics is one threat to HK's identity. Another is language. Like many Hong Kongers, he worries that the territory's predominant language, Cantonese, is being supplanted by a standardised version of Chinese used in the Mainland, known as Mandarin. At the same time, he fears that the traditional Chinese written characters that are used in Hong Kong will be pushed out by the simplified characters that are used in the Mainland.

With this threat to their language comes a threat to Hong Kong's culture, which for many Hong Kongers is deeply intertwined with Cantonese and traditional characters.

'If we can't do anything in the next few years then Hong Kong is over. It's really the last chance for us,' he said. 'Ten years later, when my children go to school, I fear they will only be able to speak Mandarin and read simplified Chinese and can't even speak Cantonese. Then what should I do? Take them out of school?'

Lee was born one year after the Tiananmen Square massacre in Beijing in 1989. The vicious crackdown on students campaigning for political reform dashed the hopes of many in Hong Kong, including Lee's father, about the handover of the territory to Chinese control in 1997. They had wanted to believe that China was on the road to becoming a freer, more open and democratic – as well as more prosperous – nation and that the absorption of Hong Kong would help to accelerate political and economic reform throughout. Even though Lee's father was greatly disappointed, he still wished his son would see a greater future for Hong Kong and China so he gave him a Chinese name that incorporates the word 'hope'.

'This name means he has hope in our generation and when we grow up and the time comes, things will get better, because we'll be more educated and know more about the world,' Lee explained. 'I share the same goal as my dad. Even though it's very hard to keep the values we cherish in Hong Kong, if we have the will and everyone tries, there's still a chance for us to succeed.'

Despite the weight of his name and his love for Chinese history and culture, Lee acknowledges that a bright future for Hong Kong does not necessarily mean a great future for the rest of China. In fact, he believes that his dream of full democracy for Hong Kong will only be satisfied if the Communist party falls from power or faces other calamities that force its hand. 'For the coming few years, what we should do is make ourselves stronger, that's the only way,' he said. 'When the Chinese economy collapses, we can take the lead.'

*

It was just after midnight one Sunday in November 2015 when Kwong Po-yin, an emergency room doctor, got the news and turned to embrace a colleague, looking tired and emotional.[8] A level-headed clinician, Kwong worked at a government hospital and had the resilience and dark humour needed to make it through countless night shifts. Now, however, she faced a very different challenge, as the first of the democratic campaigners inspired by the Occupy movement to win elected office.

Dubbed an 'Umbrella Soldier' by the Hong Kong press, she had beaten a veteran pro-Beijing politician by just thirty-nine votes to win election as a district councillor in Kowloon City. Then twenty-nine years of age, she represented a newly formed political party called Youngspiration, which was opposed to Beijing's tightening grip on Hong Kong and determined to strengthen the Hong Kong identity among young people. Her victory presaged a much wider political shift in the Legislative Council elections a year later. (The colleague Kwong hugged when her election was confirmed was an unknown 24-year-old former administrator called Yau Wai-ching. Yau failed to get elected as a district councillor that night but would succeed in securing a place in the Legislative Council in 2016, setting off a firestorm that made her briefly one of the most infamous people in Hong Kong.)

Like many others in the movement, Kwong was not political by nature. She did not grow up reading biographies of great leaders, participating in debating clubs or dreaming of power. Rather, she was propelled into politics by the forces that could tear Hong Kong apart at the seams. To understand how this happened, I went to her constituency office in the Hung Hom district of Kowloon.

She was running half an hour late after an event at a local school. As she arrived, she had to battle her way past an irate constituent who was bending her ear over the 'unhygienic' state of the public areas in her apartment complex. 'I have to deal with a lot of these kinds of problems now,' she said, with a rueful smile. 'Noise late at night, leaking pipes, writing recommendation letters, helping fill up forms . . . it's a little bit of everything.'

Kwong was used to dealing with difficult customers in her day job. Working in the emergency room, she usually sees forty patients a day, with complaints varying from the common cold to terminal illnesses. The worst cases are the pushy patients, who will start banging on the door of a treatment room asking why she is doing a resuscitation rather than treating their sore throat. 'That makes you frustrated,' she said. 'I spend a lot of time dealing with all this. But just because of those annoying and abusive people, you can't turn them all away.'

So how did this sense of responsibility take her from the emergency room to the council chamber? First came Occupy. Like Kelvin Lee, the insurance broker, Kwong was in the streets when the first tear gas canisters were fired. She helped to provide first aid. 'All the things you can imagine, or not imagine, happened that night,' she recalled. 'What impressed me most was two young girls, secondary school students I guess, holding each other and crying. They were not afraid. They were just asking each other why the government is treating them like this when they are doing something good for Hong Kong.'

She describes the Umbrella Revolution as an

epiphany. If teenagers are willing to fight so bravely for the cause, then adults should step up as well, Kwong thought. 'We can't just sit there and hope there will be someone to save us,' said the doctor.

Kwong believes Hong Kong faces three main, inter-linked problems. Firstly, an 'invasion' of people from Mainland China, which is straining public services and threatening Hong Kong's way of life. Secondly, a decline in social mobility driven by the territory's dwindling economic prospects and the failure of the self-interested political and business elite to act. And lastly, the diminution of the values and freedoms that make Hong Kong distinct from China.

I was taken aback by her anger toward Chinese immigrants in Hong Kong. It was visceral, much like the anti-immigration sentiments sweeping other parts of the world, from supporters of Donald Trump to backers of Britain's exit from the European Union. 'The influx today is too large and social services are not capable of making them dissolve well in society,' she said. 'They have condensed and become something solid.'

Like so many other people I talked to, she felt that the majority of Mainlanders were unwilling or unable to understand Hong Kong's values and culture. In a similar way to Joshua Wong and the student leaders, she saw democracy and freedom as fundamental to the Hong Kong identity and the essence of the city itself.

By contrast, she felt that many Mainlanders only saw Hong Kong as a place to hide their money, educate their kids or find trusted sources of baby milk powder, vaccines and other medicines. Echoing the complaints of many Hong Kongers about Mainland visitors and residents, she continued, with a heavy sigh: 'We spent years teaching them not to throw litter on the floor and how to protect the environment but to break this we just need five years or even less. Thirty years ago, people thought we have to allow time for China to improve so that by 2047, they will become a better place and we can integrate better. But we can see China is not improving. We are just deteriorating to match with them.'

In the first two decades after the handover, Hong Kong profited handsomely as it piggy-backed on the breakneck growth that transformed large swathes of China. Kwong's own father was one of the many Hong Kong traders who capitalised on the territory's role as a middleman, buying cheap Chinese-made goods and shipping them around the world courtesy of Hong Kong's tax- and tariff-free port. Kwong, and many others of her generation, feel that these profits accrued to a narrow slice of Hong Kong society, namely the baby boomer generation and those in the tight-knit political and business elite.

Her vision of Hong Kong is pretty bleak, and Kwong

feels that the worst is yet to come. She was able to make her own way in life by studying hard and becoming a doctor. Today she worries that medicine and other professions will become increasingly hard to enter because of the intense fight for university places. 'The ones who control the system, all their kids study overseas in boarding schools, or in international schools in Hong Kong,' Kwong said. 'They are using the ultrasound [of their baby] to get a place in the playgroup and then when you get into the playgroup you have to think of the kindergarten.'

Meanwhile, to her disgust, establishment politicians tell young Hong Kongers that if they want to escape the city's problems, they must seize career opportunities in the Mainland. 'Now they're shutting the door and saying if you can't do anything, go to China,' she said. 'But people in Hong Kong are not easy come, easy go. This is our place.'

In these circumstances, Kwong believes that whatever the practicalities, independence has become a 'natural call' for young Hong Kongers. In her view, young people see no way to disentangle the socio-economic difficulties they face from the political fact that they are, in effect, a colony of China, just like they used to be a British colony. So long as Generation HK cannot determine their political destiny through the ballot box, Kwong, Joshua Wong and the other radicals I talked to are channelling their energy into promoting the Hong Kong identity and the idea of a Hong Kong nation distinct from China.

'Many years ago, when I was in primary school, I once believed that "One Country, Two Systems" can work fine,' she said. 'But after 19 years, I can tell you it is only a gimmick. It is not for the good of Hong Kong.'

Kwong's vision of a Hong Kong rent asunder by China is dark. She says she is not 'brave enough' to have children in a society like this. She hopes her political campaigning can help improve the prospects for her friends' children. Starting with her community work, she believes she can show older generations of Hong Kongers that young people are willing to work for a better future, rather than simply demand that their Utopian ideals be respected and accepted. She also wants to help develop the Hong Kong identity, as she sees it. By spreading the idea that Hong Kongers are a free-thinking, independent-minded and fair people, who have different needs and desires from the rest of China, she hopes to lay the ground for a more autonomous future, if not full independence.

For twenty years before and after the handover, the Hong Kong and Chinese governments have tried to foster a greater sense of Chinese-ness to smooth the territory's eventual integration into the Mainland. Now, Kwong said, it is the time to start building the Hong

Kong nation and for people to discover what it means to be a Hong Konger for themselves, by separating their nation from its big brother. 'We have to spend some time to reinforce the Hong Kong identity and remind people that we can do it,' she said.

*

These intensifying political divisions in Hong Kong have pushed a growing number of young people, including a handful of professionals, in a more radical political direction. Still some, like Gary Wong, feel that the only way out of the impasse is to take a more moderate approach.

While I approached the vast majority of the people interviewed in this book, Wong came to me, in early 2016. An Oxford University graduate who won a prestigious UK government scholarship, the 33-year-old had recently quit his job as a deputy head of sales for a Hong Kong-based company that manufactures inks, paints and other chemicals in China. He was planning to run in the Legislative Council elections for a new, middle-of-the-road party called Path of Democracy. His campaign manager, who was on temporary leave from a global PR firm, wanted him to reach out to the international media.

When I met Wong later, during the thick of the election campaign, I was not convinced that he had much chance at the ballot box. He was too slick, with his tight-fitting suit giving away his recent salesman past. But he spoke with genuine concern about the polarisation in Hong Kong. 'Right now, unfortunately, politics is about dividing people,' he said, at his small campaign office in Fortress Hill in Hong Kong island, where he was going head to head with Nathan Law of Demosistō.

He saw himself as a moderate who could form a bridge between all sides from independence advocates to the Hong Kong establishment and the Beijing government itself. He was trying to force a rethink of the dichotomy that seemed to frame much of the debate about the city's future: between democratic Hong Kongers, on one side, and the unyielding Chinese government and its local agents on the other. 'Having dialogue doesn't mean we have to sacrifice our values and our bottom line,' he said.

Wong shared many of the concerns of other young Hong Kongers about housing prices, declining social mobility and a lack of democracy. Contrary to many, however, he argued that radical actions, from street occupations to supporting independence, would only further anger Beijing and lead to a greater crackdown on Hong Kong's way of life and its remaining freedoms. Wong also believed that such extreme approaches would never win the support of the quiet majority, who the radicals prefer to call 'Hong Kong pigs'. They may like the idea of democracy and want to protect Hong Kong's autonomy but they are not willing to speak themselves or encourage actions that might harm their short-term economic position. 'Some of my friends who are working in banks or other professional sectors are well aware of the situation but are silent,' he said. He explained this to me by describing how they would read and think about the problems facing Hong Kong, but they will not even discuss these issues on Facebook. This is because they fear that the Chinese and international companies that employ them will sack them or block them from promotions. 'Those are our target supporters,' he explained. 'But it's not easy to get them to speak up or get involved in campaign work.'

Wong himself has always been interested in politics and his career goals may explain in part why he takes a more moderate approach. Having completed a master's degree in diplomatic studies at Oxford in 2013, he wanted to parlay his academic and business experience into a political career. His ambition came from the sense of possibility that he felt, growing up in what he calls humble surroundings in the new town of Tuen Mun in the New Territories, with his father a policeman and his mother a housewife.

Throughout the 1980s and '90s Wong felt that life was getting steadily better. 'It was wonderful growing up in Hong Kong then,' he said. 'The 1980s was the best period in Hong Kong history. It was full of opportunities. My parents were working very hard and our family conditions improved year by year.' Most importantly, he added, it was much easier to climb the social ladder back then.

After studying translation at the University of Hong Kong, the city's leading tertiary institution, Wong joined Accenture, the management consultancy firm, in India for a year, before becoming a management trainee at the chemical company in Hong Kong. Having studied and worked in the UK, India and Mainland China, his outlook is naturally more outwardly oriented than the likes of Kelvin Lee and Kwong Po-yin. In fact, he worries that the growing promotion of the distinct 'Hong Kong identity' and the drive to protect Cantonese may have the unintended consequence of making young people uncompetitive in international terms by undermining their ability to speak English and Mandarin. That risks damaging the city's reputation as a global business centre and, counter-intuitively, making it harder for Hong Kong to reduce its economic reliance on China. Wong accepts that the question of identity in today's Hong Kong is problematic, even in the case of someone as clear-headed as himself.

'I'm a Hong Konger and a Chinese but not Chinese and a Hong Konger,' he said. More broadly, he believes that the generation that has come of age since the handover wants to 'redefine the identity of Hong Kong', even if the end goal is not exactly clear. He warns that only political compromise, rather than an identity politics that pits Hong Kong against China, can secure a better future for the city and its young citizens.

It was a testament to the divisions that so troubled Wong that his brand of middle-of-the-road-ism did not succeed at the polls. He won just 10 000 votes, too short of what he needed to get elected and far behind the 50 000 votes secured by Nathan Law.

Regardless of their political differences, and in their own different ways, Gary Wong, Kwong Po-yin and Kelvin Lee all stood up to fight for a better Hong Kong. It remains to be seen whether they are the exception to the rule among young professionals or if they are the vanguard of a new cohort with the experience and gravitas to spread democratic ideals to a wider portion of the population. But the voices of these young professionals will be crucial in the struggle to define what it means to be a Hong Konger.

One thing is for certain: these self-made professionals are more likely to provide convincing leadership to the hard-working people of Hong Kong than the traditional elite. The city's tycoons and their Generation HK offspring, who are taking up positions of increasing power in their family business empires, see their own roles – and identity – through a very different lens.

IV

The Rich Kids

Having heard so many young Hong Kongers lambast the self-interested, aloof elite, I thought that I had better find out for myself about the offspring of the city's tycoons. But the problem with detached, self-serving billionaires is that they tend to be detached and self-serving. Getting to them, via their ranks of public relations advisers and secretaries, was the first challenge. Getting them to talk openly and honestly about the problems facing Hong Kong was a much bigger task, even if I promised not to use their names.

After sending dozens of emails and making countless phone calls and entreaties to their handlers, I set up a series of meetings with younger members of some of Hong Kong's wealthiest families. Their grandparents had mostly been born in Guangdong or other parts of southern China close to Hong Kong. They had fled the poverty, political turmoil and violence of the Mainland in the early twentieth century hoping to make a better life in British-controlled Hong Kong. They had been incredibly successful, parlaying the profits from small factories and trading businesses into sprawling conglomerates spanning property, financial services, retail and more. From Li Ka-shing, Hong Kong's richest man, to the Kwok brothers, the Cheng family and Lee Shau-kee, they control vast tracts of the Hong Kong economy.

Take Li Ka-shing, who had a net worth of more than US$30 billion in 2016, according to *Forbes*, the American business magazine that compiles rich lists. His family's companies touch everything you do in Hong Kong – and take a cut accordingly. You might live in one of the many apartment complexes built by his Cheung Kong Property Holdings and work in a skyscraper owned by it. You might subscribe to his Three network for mobile phone reception and his son's PCCW for your home broadband and cable television. Li's Hong Kong Electric provides all the power to Hong Kong island. You might shop in his big supermarket chain, Park N Shop, or his pharmacy and beauty chain Watson's. A significant proportion of everything else you consume has probably come through Hong Kong port, parts of which his companies control, or the many other ports they own around the world.

With such riches behind them, the offspring of these tycoons have no struggles getting into university, getting a good job or buying a decent home, unlike most of their compatriots. Yet, life in the wake of a billionaire has its own complications. Whatever these rich kids do in business will be almost invisible in the shadow of their forefathers' achievements. But they still face the pressure of carrying on the family name and sustaining its wealth. Meanwhile, far removed from the lives of ordinary Hong Kongers, they are mercilessly mocked for their foibles in the city's raucous tabloid press.

Meeting with tycoon offspring number one was held at the American Club, one of several private members' establishments where these types like to hang out. The scion of a well-known property developer, in his mid-30s, he had invited me to lunch at McKay's, the club's steakhouse, which is situated on the upper floors of a downtown skyscraper. We agreed beforehand that I would not name him or give clues as to his identity. Still, he asked his PR advisor to sit in on our conversation to prevent any mishaps.

In these exclusive surroundings, he was keen to tell me about his enthusiasm for sustainable development. My heart sank as he repeated platitude after platitude about the need for 'smart city' designs and apartment complexes that emphasise 'liveability' and 'balance'. As always in such situations, I hoped that the early flow of non-confrontational conversation and wine would lubricate him for a more effusive exchange later.

I was wrong. Sensing our time running out, I jumped in: How concerned are you about the political divisions in Hong Kong and the deep frustrations felt by young people? He grimaced and turned to his PR advisor, who mirrored his face, sycophantically. 'Erm, politics is not really my strong point,' came the lame answer. 'I'm trying to make a difference by making sure we build the best property projects we can.' I pushed him, You must have a view on what is happening to Hong Kong? And will the political trajectory of the territory not have a huge impact on your business?

Capitulating briefly, he offered the standard line of the Hong Kong elite on Occupy and the burgeoning independence movement. 'Well I think a lot of young people's unhappiness is driven by the high cost of housing, so if only the government will release more land for development or build more affordable apartments, then we can move forward,' he said, with not the least of conviction.

As I revved up my follow-up question, the PR adviser hurriedly gestured for a waiter to bring the bill, keen to draw the encounter to a close and spare her boss any more probing. Come on, I said, Do you not think that the problems in Hong Kong have gone well beyond bread-and-butter issues to fundamental questions of identity, democracy and equality? 'If all these young people had flats, I'm sure they would stop protesting,' he responded.

It reminded me of the line apocryphally attributed to Marie Antoinette, the French queen before the revolution of 1789. When told that the peasants had no bread, the story goes, she advised: 'let them eat cake'. When Hong Kong's aristocrats are told that the people have no democracy, their response amounts to little more than: 'let them have affordable housing'. Unlike the haughty queen, who would never deign to produce cake, these guys also want to win the government contracts to construct said housing.

Hoping to find other young members of the business elite who were more in tune with the rest of Generation HK, I rushed to arrange my next meeting. Tycoon offspring number two also wanted to meet at his club. This time, it was the poshest of them all: the Hong Kong Club. The night before our breakfast meeting he called to warn me of a few things. I was told to wear a jacket and tie and not to bring a dictaphone, pen, paper or any business cards. I could bring a mobile phone but was not allowed to take it out of my pocket or look at it, let alone make a call. Without the usual tools of my trade, it was clear this was to be another off-the-record meeting. Thankfully, this chap came prepared with some more interesting opinions.

Over scrambled eggs and coffee served by a suitably obsequious waiter ('The usual, sir?'), he admitted that he despaired for the future of Hong Kong. 'Most young people have grown to hate China so much that they are really cutting off their own economic future,' he explained to me while I was forced to make mental notes, which I scribbled down afterwards in a nearby park. 'If they don't want to learn Mandarin, work in the Mainland or do business with China, what else will they do?' While he did not share their desire for such things as genuine universal suffrage and free speech, he was also none-too-pleased with the way China had responded. 'They are just exacerbating the problem and we're now locked in a vicious circle of protest and reprisal,' he said.

Could he suggest any possible ways out of the impasse? Only for his own young children, who like him had the benefit of a foreign passport, in addition to their Hong Kong one. 'I've told them not to expect that there will be much of the family business left in Hong Kong by the time they are ready to take over,' he said. 'So they better make sure they are set up for an international life.'

*

Fed up with anonymous rich kids and their blasé attitude toward the question of what it means to be a Hong Konger in the post-handover period, I was close to giving up my search when a friend suggested I talk to Lau Ming-wai. Lau is the son of one of Hong Kong's most controversial billionaires. His father, Joseph Lau, is a fugitive from justice in neighbouring Macau, another semi-autonomous Chinese territory, where he was convicted of bribery and money laundering in 2014. With a net worth of around US$15 billion, Lau senior has a penchant for younger women and the world's finest diamonds.

He does little to soften his public image. He took out a full-page advertisement on the front page of several Hong Kong newspapers in 2016 to announce that he had broken up with his ex-girlfriend – and mother of his two infant children – and that he would not be extending her any more financial support after providing her with 'money, jewellery and other gifts' to the tune of HK$2 billion (US$260 million).

Lau junior is a rather different character, known for his direct style, willingness to learn new things and more humble approach to life. While his father collects gemstones at a cost of tens of millions of dollars each, Lau is collecting careers. Now aged 35, he has a PhD in law from King's College London and describes himself as 'half an academic'. He also trained as a chartered financial analyst, working at Goldman Sachs, the investment bank, and is a registered attorney in New York. When he was living in the UK, he trained to be a flight instructor at a civilian flying club at the now-shuttered Royal Air Force base in Lyneham. Lau took over as chairman of the family's property group, Chinese Estates Holdings, at the age of 33 following his father's bribery conviction. The following year, in 2015, he was appointed as chairman of the government's commission on youth, which has the unenviable task of helping develop a youth policy that works. In 2017, he became a political adviser to Carrie Lam, who was appointed by Beijing as the new chief executive of Hong Kong from July onwards.

Lau asked me to meet him at the offices of the Bauhinia Foundation Research Centre, a government-friendly think-tank of which he is vice-chairman, among the many hats he wears. The humdrum office is located in a skyscraper that Chinese Estates had recently sold to a Mainland company for US$1.6 billion. Lau's personal PR adviser was waiting for me there, planning to sit in on the meeting. She need not have bothered because it soon became clear that nothing was off limits.

After about ten minutes, he came in, wearing a dark suit, white shirt and blue tie, sans entourage and even carrying his own backpack. Speaking in a mid-Atlantic accent, he was a smooth customer. In our initial exchange, he made it clear that he knew my boss by first name, went to university with another colleague of mine and was an 'avid reader' of the newspaper for which I work. We met a couple of days after the Legislative Council vote, in which Nathan Law was one of six candidates aged 40 or less who were elected after calling for independence or self-determination for Hong Kong.

What did Lau make of the results? His response surprised me. It showed a level of subtlety and self-awareness that had been lacking in almost every government official or pro-Beijing businessperson I had met since I moved to Hong Kong. 'What happened is encouraging on several fronts,' he said. 'I've been doing the Youth Commission chairman role for the last eighteen months and have been yakking and yakking at young people about civic participation and civic responsibilities. My view has always been that the most effective way to effect change is through the ballot box.'

Although he did not share their enthusiasm for Hong Kong's secession from China, he was keen to understand why so many had supported these six new legislators, rather than just dismissing them as cranks or traitors. In his view, they were elected because they identified and carved out a niche in the market of public opinion. 'So one has to ask why is there a market for discussion or advocacy for independence or separation,' he said. 'It's a very complex combination of identity and culture, recent history, education policy and the economic situation.'

Lau has carefully cultivated his public image to portray a fun-loving, straight shooter who can talk to all, perhaps with an eye on higher office later. His slickly produced personal website features videos of him brewing craft beer, putting on scary make-up for Halloween and chilling with two Hong Kong MCs as they rap about him ('It's the CoY, with the Ming to the Wai' is the first line of this ditty about the Commissioner of Youth). The juxtaposition between his establishment roots and his down-with-the-kids projection is awkward. Lau found that out to his discomfort a couple of months later while chairing a youth forum with CY Leung, Hong Kong's then leader, who was sworn at in front of the TV cameras by one of the excitable, young participants.

The young billionaire does seem genuinely frustrated with the failure of the political class in Hong Kong and Beijing to see the reality that is staring them in the face. 'You can say [separatism] is contravening article blah blah blah of the Basic Law, you can say this is contravening this and that but it doesn't really address why they're doing that,' he said. 'To really quell this, to really pacify what they don't like happening, it takes more than denying and condemnation.'

For Lau, there are three main forces propelling the rapid growth of the separatist movement: identity, socio-economic inequality and China's cack-handed approach to young people in Hong Kong. With regards to the first point, he explained that Generation HK, himself included, had grown up in an 'identity vacuum', where they felt neither Chinese nor British. So young people are redefining who they are and imagining a new Hong Kong identity.

Like many others in Hong Kong, he felt no allegiance to Britain while growing up. 'We had these black passports with the unicorn and horse on it or whatever but we were not attached to the British identity,' he explained. On the night of the handover, 30 June 1997, young people 'didn't feel much about identity, Chinese or British. Just blah.' But after 1997, he contended, the Hong Kong government and the Beijing authorities did not do enough to fill this vacuum, so negative sentiments toward the Mainland started to seep in. This 'them and us' sentiment then began to ferment before 'exploding exponentially' as Hong Kong was shaken up over the last five years. Part of the problem is that many Hong Kongers have experienced a huge shock in their status relative to their Mainland cousins.

'Hong Kongers went from looking down on them in the 1970s and 1980s as being less civilised, rude, uneducated peasants to, in the post-handover period, not being sure how to view them,' he said. Now after several decades of rapid growth, Hong Kongers are struggling to accept that Mainlanders are 'no longer peasants, they're rich bastards in Rolls-Royces.'

A city apart, Hong Kong has long been defined in contrast to the rest of China. Orderly when China was chaotic. Free when China was repressed. Rich when

China was poor. But, on the economic front, the equation has changed. And just like the anxious high-school and university students who fear competition from their Mainland peers, Hong Kong's self-confidence has been shaken by China's economic transformation.

Able to afford plenty of Rolls-Royces himself, Lau accepts that socio-economic inequality within Hong Kong is also a significant problem. 'Our political and business leaders in Hong Kong and in China talk continuously about the economic benefits that China has brought to Hong Kong,' he said. The trouble is that the benefits all went to a narrow group of people, including himself. 'The business community may have benefited a lot,' he said. 'Joe Public's standard of living, Joe Public's wage growth, has no relation to GDP growth.' This divide between 'Joe Public', to use Lau's Americanism, and the Hong Kong elite is just as sharp as the perceived divide between Hong Kong and China.

The third driver of youth alienation is the attitude taken by Communist leaders in Beijing, not a group of people that many other establishment figures in Hong Kong are willing to criticise publicly or privately. 'The way Chinese officials speak about Hong Kong issues, the way that Hong Kong-China relations are promoted, the way they condemn various movements or issues, their method and style are all counter-productive,' said Lau. Having not faced a proper political contest since winning the civil war against Chiang Kai-shek's Nationalists in 1949, he argues that the Communist Party has forgotten how to win public support and has become too reliant on its big stick.

The result in Hong Kong is a kind of Communist propaganda-lite. Hong Kong and Chinese officials opt for platitudes, condemnations and stonewalling over a real debate about questions of identity and the future of the city. The attempts at more gentle persuasion come in the form of free trips to see the Great Wall, the Terracotta Army and other examples of China's historical might, alongside Potemkin village-style tours of model factories and research centres. This stilted approach has merely pushed Generation HK away, further entrenching its opposition to the Communist party's idea of what it means to be Chinese. 'The soft skills of promotion, persuasion, winning hearts and minds, self-deprecation – this sort of stuff is not a well-practised craft in Mainland China,' Lau said.

As Nathan Law's headmaster found out to his misfortune, the Communist hard-sell does not work in Hong Kong, where the internet is unrestricted and people still enjoy a high degree of free speech, unlike in the Mainland. 'Our young people aren't stupid, so you instantly fail on that ground,' said Lau. 'We, Hong Kong Joe Public, receive information at a frequency and channel much closer to the Western than the Chinese style.

So when you broadcast information using the China frequency, we don't receive much of it, and it looks like it's something from another planet.' As he raises taboo after taboo, I wonder why Lau is being so openly critical.

Despite – or because of – his upbringing, he has always done things his own way. His CV is long enough to make even the most accomplished of polymaths feel like they have wasted their life. Lau has been interested in politics since he was a 'little kid', although not, he added with a wry smile, 'to the Joshua Wong extent'. This begged the question - does he see his current position as a stepping stone to higher office? He demurred.

'The proper question is who would want to join either the zoo that is known as the Legislative Council or the fire-pit known as government,' he said. 'Look at where I am now. I'm a non-official chairman of a seemingly important advisory body. And if they have to mention my father, I've got tons of money. I seem to be straddling, one foot kind of within government, one foot outside. Would I be able to speak to you this freely if I was a proper member of the government? Probably not.'

Unable to push him any further on the issue, I close by asking him where he thinks Hong Kong is heading and find that he is not overly optimistic. 'If you extrapolate from the last ten years, then where it's going is pretty horrible, let's face it,' he said. 'There are a lot of people from all across society and all across the political spectrum who realise this and are trying to do something about it.' But, he admits, so far the political responses have been 'very ineffective'.

Part of the problem is that no-one in the establishment, apart from him it seems, is willing to talk about it, precisely because they know how bad things are. 'No one in their right mind will go out in public and say this is where it's going,' he said, with a self-deprecatory chuckle. Not only does the establishment not want to talk about what is happening to Hong Kong, it is starting to curb the public discussion of such sensitive matters. It is aping the soft repression practised by Singapore, where the government has developed a much smoother form of authoritarianism than China's Communists.

To understand this squeezing of the public space for political discussion, I went to speak to some of the free minds of Generation HK: artists who have been on the receiving end of the authorities' increasing censorship. The most memorable artists always try to put the establishment on edge, pushing the boundaries of acceptability and forcing societies to question their preconceptions about identity and meaning. In these troubled times in Hong Kong, the political class is pushing back just as hard. This battle to maintain freedom of expression is central to how many young Hong Kongers see their city, as a rare bastion of creativity and liberty within China.

V

The Banned Artists

In the piercing sunlight, an old woman struggles up the steep hill to the British consulate-general in Hong Kong, which sits just above the Pacific Place mall in the city centre. Wearing sandals, black trousers and a flowery red shirt, she looks like many other Hong Kong grandmothers. But she is a woman on a very specific mission. In her right hand, she holds an umbrella that she uses for support, like a walking stick. In her left, is a metal can. Stopping in front of the British royal seal – 'Dieu and Mon Droit' or 'God and my Right' – she closes her eyes and grimaces as she pours the can's contents over her hair. Then she crouches, stares up at the sun one last time, takes a lighter from her pocket, ignites it and is consumed in a ball of flames. A final act of protest and self-sacrifice in support of the young Hong Kongers fighting for their freedoms.

The scene haunted Hong Kongers and so disturbed supporters of the Chinese government that they quickly went to work to stop the images spreading – even though they were only from a fictional movie, titled *Ten Years*.

China's Communist leaders fear self-immolations, for they show that their critics are not mere rabble-rousers or agents paid by foreign forces but people willing to die for their cause. I witnessed it for myself when I visited Tiananmen Square to report on the annual meeting of China's rubber-stamp parliament, the National People's Congress. The government had deployed mobile fire-fighters principally for the purpose of deterring and, if necessary, dousing would-be self-immolators. Dressed in jumpsuits with fire-extinguisher backpacks, they looked like an Orwellian version of the Ghostbusters from the eponymous film.

'Self-immolation' was one of five short stories that comprised *Ten Years*, a low-budget film by a bunch of young Hong Kong directors that imagined what the city would look like in 2025. Released at the end of 2015, it became an unexpected hit at the few cinemas showing it, won the best movie prize at Hong Kong's annual film awards and then promptly disappeared from screens.

It was not just the self-immolation storyline that resonated. The other short stories featuring a Cultural Revolution-style crackdown on sensitive books, the central government manipulating local politics to bring in harsh security laws and restrictions on the use of Cantonese in favour of Mandarin also struck a chord with Hong Kongers.

Made with a budget of just HK$500 000 (US$64 000) and the help of many unpaid volunteers, *Ten Years* was not going to win much praise for its cinematography. But that was not the point. I went to watch the movie at the Cinematheque, one of the few cinemas that show independent films in Hong Kong. Voracious eaters at the best – and worst – of times, the Hong Kongers in the audience soon put down their nachos and popcorn and watched in stunned silence, breaking into tears during the self-immolation scene and at the end of the film. *Ten Years* came at a particularly raw time for a city that has been worrying about its future for decades.

In the months before it was released, five employees from a Hong Kong bookseller based in the Causeway Bay area disappeared mysteriously. Causeway Bay Books published and sold works that were highly critical of the Communist Party in China, from weighty historical tomes to screeds that recycled unsubstantiated gossip about top leaders including Xi Jinping. Several months later, the all-powerful Chinese security forces admitted that they had detained them. The case of the Causeway Bay booksellers, whose store remains shuttered, shocked Hong Kong and sent a bitter chill through the once-thriving publishing industry. Hong Kongers feared that the Chinese government was intensifying its crackdown on their rights in the wake of the Occupy protests a year earlier. *Ten Years* spoke to these concerns in an intimate way. As life appeared to be imitating art, the dark joke soon became that the film should be renamed One Year or even This Year.

The Global Times, an influential tabloid newspaper that is owned by the Chinese Communist Party's main mouthpiece, the *People's Daily*, described *Ten Years* as a 'virus of the mind' that Hong Kongers should reject.[9] Cinemas soon did. Although *Ten Years* was selling out in the few screens showing it, in February 2016, they suddenly removed it.

In April, when the movie won the top prize at the Hong Kong Film Awards, Chinese broadcasters decided to drop their coverage of the ceremony and the Mainland media churlishly omitted it from lists of the award-winners. Several months later I went to meet Ng Ka-leung and Jevons Au, the mastermind behind *Ten Years* and a director of one of the five shorts, respectively. Au's office was located on the sixth floor of one of many warren-like industrial buildings in Lai Chi Kok, in Kowloon, where artists, entrepreneurs and others come in search of less expensive rents. Sitting on a sofa, surrounded by film posters, books and DVDs, I asked these two thoughtful young film-makers what had happened to the film.

The cinemas told Au they had dropped the film for 'commercial reasons', even though it was selling out until it disappeared and they knew that more and more people wanted to see it as word spread. 'What's the real reason behind it? Perhaps they didn't want to get into trouble,' he said. Throwing his hands up in resignation and laughing he added: 'we don't know and we'll never know'. These budding filmmakers were deeply frustrated. Having created that rare film that generates critical acclaim and decent box-office takings, they had run into an almost immediate dead-end.

Hong Kong has long prided itself on being a special enclave in the Chinese world, thanks to the substantial freedoms it has enjoyed relative to the Communist-ruled Mainland. In the past, dissidents, artists and writers could freely discuss matters and create works that would be deemed taboo or even criminal in the Mainland. Historian Jeffrey Wasserstrom has called it the 'West Berlin of China'.[10] The creative energy stemming in part from these freedoms gave the world artists like Bruce Lee and Jackie Chan, John Woo and Wong Kar-wai. It also helped promote a thriving publishing industry that produced a wide range of Chinese books that would be banned in the Mainland. The vanishing of *Ten Years*, alongside the disappearance of the booksellers, were clear signs that things were changing, for the worse.

China's Communist leaders realise that film is a powerful mass medium that they need to control in order to manage the perceptions of their own people and the outside world. Beijing already tightly restricts the number of foreign films that can be shown in China and bans those that feature content or artists that are critical of their rule such as Free Tibet campaigners like Richard Gere. Meanwhile, films that portray Chinese history or modern China in a positive light are given favourable treatment.

With China predicted soon to overtake the US as the world's biggest movie market, many in Hollywood are willing to do whatever it takes to get access to their share of bulging Chinese consumer wallets. As powerful Chinese conglomerates like Dalian Wanda and China Media Capital spend billions of dollars buying up Western cinema chains and film studios, movie-making with Chinese characteristics is being exported to the rest of the world. The Beijing government codified this crackdown in a new film law implemented in November 2016. It banned Chinese companies from collaborating with foreign individuals and organisations that engage in 'activities damaging China's national dignity, honour and interests, or harming social stability or hurting national feelings'.[11] A resurgent China under President Xi's leadership wants to police depictions of China well beyond its jurisdiction, starting with Hong Kong, which was supposedly guaranteed autonomy and freedom of speech and expression.

The struggles of Jevons Au, Ng Ka-lueng and other Hong Kong artists are a harbinger of how the rise of China will change the rules of the game globally. Neither of these directors, who are both thirty-five years of age, and thus familiar with the struggles of Generation HK, see themselves as martyrs to a higher political cause. They neither expected the film to be so popular, nor so loathed by the powers-that-be. Modishly dressed, in a blue polo shirt, white shorts and garish Adidas trainers, Au said he was driven, to a great extent, by commercial motives. Ng, who looked more professorial with a goatee and glasses, sees himself as more of an artist and curator.

'We didn't set out to make a political film,' said Ng. 'The directors and myself came together to talk about our concerns and our observations on the Hong Kong situation.' He felt that it was important for Hong Kongers to engage in an honest debate about what is happening to their city, rather than ignore the ground shifting beneath their feet. Many found the depiction of Hong Kong's future in the film bleak, if not terrifying. The point, Ng insisted, was to force people to face reality, rather than escape from it, in the hope that they might be able to work out a better way forward.

'People in Hong Kong are not very good at express-ing their feelings and their emotions but many cried after watching *Ten Years*,' said Au. 'It helped them to relieve their emotions and then, afterwards, they might have the power again.' With a smile, he suggested that Hong Kongers should take heart from the Chinese Communist slogan: 'Wherever there is oppression, there is resistance'.

Au admitted that the current climate of tension and suppression is good for film-makers and artists. 'But I don't want to have a good film and then live in a shit place', he added. Like many Hong Kongers, both directors said they were proud to be ethnically Chinese. But they feel that the government of the People's Republic of China is destroying their home. The previous colonial authorities were hardly keen to promote art that attacked the system or undermined British rule, Ng said. But at least they thought about what was in the long-term interests of Hong Kongers, unlike the Chinese government and its Hong Kong functionaries. 'They are just playing us for fools,' he said. Au agreed, 'In 1997, when they promised us fifty years unchanged, many people, including me, believed that. We were too naïve.'

*

China's top leaders rarely come to Hong Kong, knowing the disdain in which they are held by large portions of the city's 7 million people. Hence, the visit by Zhang

Dejiang in May 2016 was a big deal. He is the head of the National People's Congress and the third most important comrade after President Xi Jinping and Premier Li Keqiang.

The Hong Kong authorities duly made all the necessary preparations. They deployed thousands of police officers, from sniper teams atop skyscrapers to frogmen scouring the harbour for bombs; they locked down swathes of the city and even glued the pavement so disgruntled Hong Kongers could not dig up the bricks and throw them at Zhang. The cordon was so tight that Nathan Law, who would be elected to the Legislative Council just months later, was wrestled to the ground by police as he tried to approach Zhang's hotel to protest against the visit. Amid the intense security fears, no-one thought to double-check the massive art installation that was scheduled to open on the façade of Hong Kong's tallest building midway through Zhang's visit.

'Our 60-second friendship begins now' was a nine-and-a-half minute visual display that cascaded down the side of the 108-storey International Commerce Centre, which sits on the Kowloon side of Victoria Harbour. One of the world's biggest ever artworks, it had been commissioned by the government's Arts Development Council as part of an exhibition of public art designed to shed light on the 'Human Vibrations' of the city. The work, designed to make people 'cherish the moment', featured the image of a clock moving down the building, interspersed with the phrases 'I will remember this minute' and 'You can't change this fact'. In the last 90-seconds of the display, a digital clock started counting down each second from a total of more than 970 000 000 seconds – or thirty years. A typically baffling modern art project, no-one took much notice until the young local artists behind it, Sampson Wong and Jason Lam, released another work online on 18 May, a day after Zhang had arrived in Hong Kong. Called 'Countdown Machine', it included a photo of the countdown clock on the International Commerce Centre, with a brief explanation that this was a countdown to 1 July 2047, the end-date of China's pledge to Hong Kong in 1997 that 'the previous capitalist system and way of life shall remain unchanged for fifty years'.

As the artists started to talk to the media about their work, the mandarins realised what was going on. The Arts Development Council pulled the plug on the International Commerce Centre project after five days, claiming that the artists had 'changed the title and statement of their work' without permission. It was a humiliating incident. While the Hong Kong government and Zhang were trying to present a united front to Hong Kongers – and more importantly, President Xi – the artists were highlighting the real, deep anxieties felt by many residents.

'It's strange to live with two countdowns in your life,' Wong told me later. Before the handover in 1997, the Chinese government had set up a countdown clock in Tiananmen Square to celebrate the coming reunification with a part of the nation that, in their eyes, had been stolen by conniving imperialists. Many Hong Kongers were counting down too, whether excited by the prospect of shaking off the British yoke or fearful for their future. Now, as Mainland influence seemed to be growing week by week, they were already counting down to 2047. 'People are starting to compare Hong Kong with Venice and saying it will be just a very ordinary city in 2047,' said Wong, in reference to the decline of the Italian city from global trading centre to glorified museum.

Wong had asked me to meet him at a café near where he was working as a history and sociology lecturer at the Hong Kong Academy of Performing Arts. He picked a hipster joint of the sort that is rapidly becoming as widespread as Starbucks, with the wooden chairs and sofas swapped for identikit industrial chic. Dressed in a grey t-shirt, with glasses and an appropriately artistic mop of hair, he was still indignant about the removal of his work.

'It's stupid,' he said. The project was accepted by the Arts Development Council and only removed because of the interpretation he later suggested, rather than the nature of the artwork itself. Of course, Wong knew exactly what he was doing. The son of a lawyer, he was interested in politics from a young age and had studied government and public administration at the Chinese University of Hong Kong before completing a PhD in geography and urban studies at the University of Manchester. He started to dabble in protest art in 2014 after doing the most unrevolutionary of things: going to an exhibition at London's historic Victoria and Albert Museum.

Disobedient Objects, the name of the exhibition, was a wildly popular showcase for art and design produced by political activists and social movements from around the world. 'It was phenomenal,' said Wong. When tens of thousands of Hong Kongers occupied the streets and fought with the police later that year, Wong and Lam produced their own work called *Stand by You: Add Oil Machine for Hong Kong Occupiers*.

Playing on the Chinese expression 'add oil' (加油) – a term of encouragement to make an extra effort – they projected expressions of support for the protesters from around the world. Wong pointed out that the occupiers also used a how-to manual produced as part of Disobedient Objects to make masks to protect themselves against the volleys of police tear gas.

When Wong was later commissioned for the ICC project, the Hong Kong curators should have known what they were getting. The young artist was ambivalent about the consequences of his endeavours. He had succeeded in tapping into Hong Kongers' frustrations with Beijing – and exposing the contradictions of an art establishment that wanted to produce edgy work that grabbed international attention without upsetting the nervous authorities. He said that unveiling the project was like 'holding up a mirror' in front of the art world in Hong Kong. They must ask themselves if they really care about artistic freedom or just getting government grants. Wong was disappointed by the reactions. 'A lot of people I expected to be more liberal were not,' he said.

For these artists, like many of the other members of Generation HK I interviewed, the pressures on the city were forcing them to question who they were, what it meant to be a Hong Konger and where they were heading as the 50-year clock ticked down.

As Beijing tightens controls, Wong believes that Hong Kong is facing a cultural war over the space for free public expression. Given the city's legacy, he thinks that Hong Kong artists have a responsibility to fight state censorship and its more insidious cousin, self-censorship. 'Being in Hong Kong, we're in a unique and interesting position to make artworks that criticise China,' he said. 'It's a chronicle of the time we're experiencing now. If we don't do that, we're skipping one of the most important themes we should embrace.'

The speed with which the room for expression is closing has alarmed the artists and writers in Hong Kong who want to produce challenging works that open up discussion about Hong Kong's identity and its future. The dystopian *Ten Years* was deemed not safe for public consumption by cinemas early in 2016. *Yellowing*, a documentary about the Occupy movement, struggled to get commercial screenings soon afterwards. Then, in September, the Hong Kong branch of the Asia Society, a US educational organisation whose main backers include a Hong Kong property tycoon called Ronny Chan, pulled a screening of another Occupy documentary called *Raise the Umbrellas*. Plenty of underground venues remain but it is getting harder to reach broad audiences and find the funding opportunities that all but the most ardent of purists need to survive. 'There's always been a dichotomy between the market-driven and the more marginal part of the art world,' said Wong. 'For some time, the government and funding bodies were neutral, giving some space and money to fringe projects. But now they are much more cautious. If the projects touch on politics, it's much more difficult to get space, funding and public relations exposure.'

What is happening in art is just a reflection of the growing climate of fear, self-censorship and omerta. I had come to Hong Kong having previously worked in Indonesia, one of the most vibrant democracies in Asia, and Vietnam, which is usually found alongside China at the bottom of press freedom indices. I guessed that

Hong Kong would be somewhere in the middle. But my expectations were confounded, on the downside. Senior government officials were reluctant to give interviews to foreign journalists, while most in the private sector were unwilling to go on the record criticising the government. When Hong Kong's leaders like chief executive CY Leung were pressed on worrisome issues like the kidnapping of the booksellers, they gave no substantive answers about what had happened to them, leaving their people living in uncertainty.

Wong, like many, believes that the real threat is not to artists per se but to the civic liberties that make Hong Kong what it is. Holding a British passport, Wong has a get-out clause, unlike many Hong Kongers. He is thinking about moving to London. He is also trying to write a book based on his PhD research about disease in Hong Kong. Wong examined how an outbreak of the plague in 1894 was a turning point for the British colonial authorities, who had previously not meddled so heavily in the daily life of the city's Chinese citizens. 'After that, they intervened more in how life was run,' he said. 'The government used disease to take control of society.'

He sees a parallel in how Beijing and the Hong Kong government are trying to use the growing disease – as they view it – of the independence and self-determination movement to sanitise political life today. The difference, in his opinion, is that the authorities are now overreacting to a threat that is more illusory than real. 'Rationally if I look at the so-called independence movement in Hong Kong, it's very naïve,' he said. 'If they didn't do anything about it, it would just fade away.'

Yet, the harder the government has cracked down, the more people have voiced their support for Hong Kong's separation from China. The disease, as Wong referred to it, is spreading, much faster than anyone could have imagined. And advocates of independence believe that this is only the beginning.

VI

The Would-Be Revolutionaries

Edward Leung was trying painfully hard not to mention the very thing that we had met to discuss. 'I need more knowledge about economic development for Hong Kong so to convince more people that we are able to . . . ,' he said, trailing off. He sighed and started again. 'To convince more people that Hong Kong . . . how to say . . . that Hong Kong is able to be inde— . . . I couldn't say that.' How about 'self-reliant', I suggested, wanting to dig him out of his rhetorical – and legal – hole. 'Yes,' he said, laughing. 'That Hong Kong can be self-reliant.'

I had come to talk to one of the figureheads of the small and radical but fast-growing movement that is pushing for Hong Kong independence. They face an uphill battle, to say the least. Leung and his organisation, Hong Kong Indigenous, exist in limbo, the result of the government's clumsy efforts to stamp them out. Just like with Joshua Wong's Demosistō, the government has blocked HK Indigenous from establishing a legal entity. They are forced to collect donations and rent office space under the guise of an online broadcaster called *Channel i*.

When I met Leung, he had recently been banned from standing in the Legislative Council election because of his advocacy of independence. He was trying to overturn that ruling by claiming – not very convincingly – that he had changed his view on separation from China. He also had a police charge for rioting – and a possible five-year jail term – hanging over his head, with the trial not due until 2018. When I arrived at the poky rented office of HK Indigenous in Kowloon, Leung was napping on a sofa. He looked worn down by his legal and political battles, as well as the skirmishes with the pro-government journalists who follow him and other radical activists around town hoping to catch them off guard, in embarrassing situations. So Leung went for an eye-opening cigarette on the balcony before leaping into the discussion with relish.

'After 1997, along these nineteen years, we've witnessed the decline of all our core values, living style and culture,' he explained. 'The main influence is from China. They deprive our political rights, they undermine our culture. They want to control every aspect in Hong Kong.' With Hong Kong's autonomy under attack, and with Beijing unwilling to grant full democracy, calling for independence seemed like a logical next step for Leung and a growing number of young Hong Kongers. Independence was – for its advocates – the ultimate destination when the journey to build a new Hong Kong identity was complete, simply the latest of many nations that have been imagined into existence.

Polling by the respected Chinese University of Hong Kong during the summer of 2016 showed that 17 per cent of people supported independence, even though only 4 per cent regarded it as a possible outcome for the city. Generation HK were much stronger advocates of separation from China, with 39 per cent of 15 to 24-year-olds and 24 per cent of 25 to 39-year-olds behind it. Just a few years earlier, talk of independence was virtually non-existent, deemed laughable by many reasonable people, taboo by government supporters and anathema by Beijing. China's Communist rulers remain deeply fearful of threats to territorial integrity and national sovereignty, having told their 1.4 billion people that only they can defend the nation and reverse centuries of humiliation by the colonial powers. The rapid rise of the independence movement has shocked the Hong Kong and Chinese governments. And their heavy-handed response has focused even more attention on emerging leaders like Edward Leung. Tall and blessed with good looks, he emerged from relative obscurity to the forefront of a radical movement that has captivated a growing number of young Hong Kongers, ready to fight for their identity and rights.

When I spoke to Leung for the first time, he told me of his admiration for the violent resistance doctrine of Malcolm X, the US black rights campaigner. I could not decide if his talk of revolution on the streets of Hong Kong was disturbing or preposterous. I had a better idea of his intentions a couple of months later – in February 2016 – when he was charged with rioting after a night of mayhem in the busy commercial district of Mong Kok. If Joshua Wong and Agnes Chow represent the acceptable face of the anti-Beijing movement, Leung and his fellow travellers are the bad boys and girls: smoking, drinking, swearing and burning Chinese flags.

Leung admits he is worried about the prospect of going to jail. Ray Wong, the founder of Hong Kong Indigenous, and several other of his friends also face the prospect of lengthy prison sentences if convicted for their part in the 'incident', as Leung prefers to call it so as not to imply that any criminal offence has been committed. The mayhem, the worst street violence to hit Hong Kong since the 1960s, began when government food safety officials tried to crack down on unlicensed street hawkers who traditionally set up stalls during the Chinese New Year holiday. This act was seen by Leung and his friends as an attack on Hong Kongers' identity by a puppet government that was threatening local traditions.

Hong Kong Indigenous and other groups of so-called localists – who advocate a tough stance in defence of Hong Kong's way of life – came out to protect the hawkers in what the media dubbed a 'Fishball Revolution', after the popular local street snack. Scuffles broke out and the situation turned nasty as the riot police moved in, leading to hours of violence in the narrow streets of an important commercial district. Police shot round after round of tear gas and one officer even fired his pistol into the air to warn off the rioters who had downed one of his colleagues. The rioters fought back, throwing bricks, dustbins and any other missiles they could find. Looking back, Leung lamented that violence can be 'very costly'. Still, the former philosophy student at the University of Hong Kong defended his approach.

'I would not deny the importance of forceful resistance because the core thing for me is to force the government to kneel down,' he said, speaking in a soft voice that belied his militant rhetoric. 'If peaceful protest and civil disobedience works, I'd love to do so. But if it doesn't work, I need to think of another more forceful way to pressure the government.' In short, he embraces 'all means'.

Hong Kong is by and large a very peaceful place and I had expected widespread condemnation of the riot. The government – and its supporters – were unambiguous in their criticism. Yet, a surprising number of pro-democracy friends who oppose violence and separatism said they felt sympathetic toward these angry youths. It was as though this small mob was expressing something that many other young Hong Kongers felt but feared to express.

At that time, Leung was standing in a by-election for a seat in the Legislative Council and most analysts presumed that this little-known activist would be punished at the polls for his alleged role in the rioting. To everyone's amazement, his role in the 'incident' helped propel him into third place, with 66 000 votes, in a foretaste of the political earthquake that would rattle Hong Kong and Beijing later that year.

*

Independence supporters like Edward Leung and Chan Ho-tin, another student leader who founded a group called the Hong Kong National Party, underwent their formative political education during Occupy. However, unlike mainstream student activists such as Agnes Chow and Joshua Wong, they learnt a different lesson from the movement. Watching his classmates being beaten and tear-gassed by the police during the Umbrella Revolution unleashed something more visceral in Leung.

'I couldn't forget that night, I couldn't forget that night,' he said, his voice trailing off with emotion. He was shocked when he saw friends getting arrested and handcuffed, their faces and varsity hoodies stained with blood. He wanted revenge.

Chan Ho-tin, an engineering and business student, felt more frustration with the other protesters. 'I thought Occupy was somewhat meaningless,' he said. 'People just went there to sleep, singing, eating, laughing, like they were having a party.' As he pondered what he could do, a group of his friends came across the national flag of China and decided to tear it down and burn it. This act of violent defiance prompted a realisation that Hong Kongers could not simply ask the Chinese government for democracy and autonomy. They would have to take it. 'We don't need to ask for democracy from them, we can just cut off the relationship and become independent,' he said.

Meeting Leung and Chan, it was hard to believe that they could find a bigger audience for views this extreme by Hong Kong's standards. With both of their organisations effectively blacklisted by the government, they were unable to open bank accounts. Without the ability to raise more funds, it would be hard to expand beyond their small base of volunteers. Even then the Hong Kong government – and Beijing – were worried about their possible influence.

When Leung and Chan registered as candidates for September's territory-wide legislative election, officials blocked them using a tactic straight out of the Beijing playbook. Candidates already had to declare allegiance to the Basic Law, the territory's mini-constitution, and the Hong Kong Special Administration Region. So the bureaucrats conjured up a new form that required candidates to declare that Hong Kong was an inalienable part of China. Chan refused to sign it on the basis that it was not lawful – and his candidacy was rejected. Leung signed it but his candidacy was rejected after the returning officer decided that his declaration was not sincere. Both plan to appeal to the courts.

'I really want to be a legislator, I want to represent the people,' Leung said. Fatefully, he had received the email about the declaration form (which many believe was an idea hatched in Beijing), while he was in a lecture about the rise of China.

In total six candidates were blocked because of their purported support for independence. However, if the government thought it had nipped the problem in the bud, it was sorely mistaken. Under the so-called Plan B, a member of the Youngspiration party called Sixtus Leung stepped up to stand in the New Territories East seat that Edward Leung had intended to fight. A 30-year-old who had formerly worked in online marketing, Sixtus preferred to be known as Baggio Leung because his official English name was 'too hard for Hong Kong people to pronounce'. He named himself after

Roberto Baggio, the Italian footballer of the 1990s who was famous for his free-kick scoring technique and his rat-tail haircut. Baggio Leung was one of three Youngspiration candidates including Yau Wai-ching, the friend and former assistant to Dr Kwong Po-yin. Backed by Edward Leung's group and his impressive public speaking skills, Baggio made an immediate impact with voters and the press, even though he only had a matter of weeks to pull together a campaign. I went to talk to Baggio in the last week of the election campaign as he and his baby-faced volunteers pounded the streets furiously in the hope of victory.

After watching him hand out flyers and talk to morning commuters in Tseung Kwan O, a middle-class housing estate, we sat down for breakfast in a nearby shopping mall. 'Before Plan B, I planned to retire from the political world already because I want to keep Youngspiration young and I'm the oldest guy in the party already,' he said. He described Edward Leung as a 'genius' and a 'natural leader' who he wants to see become 'another Sun Yat-sen', the founder of modern Chinese nationalism and one of the few figures admired equally by China's Communists and their political opponents. Rangy and bookish, like his younger mentor Edward Leung, Baggio also talks with a passion for his cause.

'Life in Hong Kong, especially for youngsters, is very difficult,' he said. The cost of living is among the highest in the world and graduate salaries have not increased for many years. He insists these economic difficulties cannot be divorced from the political problem at the heart of Hong Kong: the people cannot elect their own leaders. 'Of course, we want bigger apartments and higher salaries,' said Baggio. 'But Hong Kongers want more than that. We treasure our freedoms but we are losing them. We want democracy and we want a system that can make Hong Kong develop sustainably.'

Mainstream opinion in Hong Kong and beyond regards independence as an impossibility because the Chinese government – and the vast majority of its people – is resolutely opposed to any threats to its sovereignty and seeks to crush separatist movements from Xinjiang to Tibet. Even many moderate supporters of democracy in Hong Kong, such as Chris Patten, the last British governor before the handover, argue that support for independence will backfire by forcing Beijing to crack down harder on the territory's freedoms and autonomy. Nonetheless, Edward Leung, Baggio Leung and their supporters see the issue very differently. They view the call for independence as an attempt to defend the essence of what Beijing promised them in the run-up to 1997. '"One Country Two Systems" was designed to protect the *independence* of Hong Kong,' said Edward Leung. 'If Hong Kong is the same as China, why do you have to use two systems to define us? People already recognised that Hong Kong is a special place.'

In this 'impossible dream' of independence, what does it mean to be a Hong Konger? 'One Country, Two Systems' was an acceptance that Hong Kong was already separated politically as well as geographically from its neighbour. For Edward Leung however, the idea of being a Hong Konger today is rooted in basic values, rather than geography and the accident of history. 'If you agree with our values, living style and culture and are willing to pledge your loyalty to this place and to preserve all this, then you are a Hong Konger', he said. 'It's very idealistic but I like this definition.'

Edward Leung was born in the Mainland, but his mother moved the family to Hong Kong when he was one. He embraces the idea of Hong Kong nationalism as a cosmopolitan, civic movement driven by shared values rather than a nativist one driven by chauvinism and xenophobia. But which values? Certainly not many would share his advocacy of violent resistance, even if they appreciated his dedication to the cause of defending Hong Kong's freedoms.

When I met Chan Ho-tin for coffee later, he agreed with Edward Leung that, despite many shared roots, 'Hong Kong people are not Chinese people'.

'We speak a different language and have a different culture, although similar,' he said. 'Our living style, rule of law, common law system . . . in many many ways we are different. So how come you can rule us? How come you can decide my life and decide my destiny? In my mind Hong Kong is just a colony of China. Before 1997, it was a colony of Britain and now we're a colony of China.'

Chan, who like Edward Leung and Baggio Leung is unusually tall for a Hong Konger, insists that Hong Kong already has many of the institutional facets of an independent state, but for the small matter of China and its sovereignty. 'We're quite ready to be a country,' he said. 'We have our own currency, our own border, our own passport, our legal system, our financial system. What we are lacking is just a government and a constitution.'

After graduating from Hong Kong Polytechnic University, Chan worked for an engineering company for a few months before quitting to focus on his abortive run for the Legislative Council. Now he spends his time giving media interviews, trying to organise a small group of supporters and, as he puts it, 'infiltrating' high schools. He claims that seventy high schools in Hong Kong have some sort of pro-independence grouping and that he provides them with leaflets and materials to help convert other pupils. 'Today they are just students but in a few years they will be professionals and will be the backbone of the whole society,' he said. Despite his geeky demeanour, Chan talks the revolutionary talk more intently than the others. I wonder how much influence he has on his young acolytes. He claims that the students could have taken control of the city on 29 September 2014, when the police backed down a day after they had fired tear gas and brought tens of thousands onto the street at the start of the Occupy movement. 'Two years ago we had so many people on the street,' he said. 'We could have disbanded the government but we were not prepared for that.'

Many feared at the time that Beijing would send in the People's Liberation Army, which has a garrison in Hong Kong, just as it had done eventually to wipe out the Tiananmen Square students in Beijing in 1989. That did not happen and Chan thinks it an unlikely response to future street actions. 'China can't easily conduct military action in Hong Kong or they will bear great consequences politically and economically,' he said.

Sitting in a Starbucks and discussing revolution over a café latte seems faintly ridiculous. But if this is all talk, it has not proved completely empty. By bringing a taboo into the public domain, Chan Ho-tin and Edward Leung laid the groundwork for a wider movement. By drawing on what many saw as unreasonable repression from the Hong Kong government and Beijing, they intensified the growing feeling of 'us versus them'. Baggio won his seat in the election, as did Yau Wai-ching. In total six lawmakers were elected to the 70-seat Legislative Council after advocating some form of self-determination or independence for Hong Kong. All forty years of age or less, together with similar-minded candidates, they won around 20 per cent of the vote on 4 September.

The result represented the rise of a whole generation of Hong Kongers with little or no fealty to China, whether for political reasons or because of how they see their own identity. Despite this, they are still divided over how to move forward and overcome the huge obstacles that are blocking their path to greater freedom and democracy. A Hong Kong nation is growing in the minds of many young people. But no-one has a realistic plan to bring this nation to life, whether as a genuinely autonomous part of China or an independent state.

In the lead-up to the election, Baggio accepted that despite the generational shift, this was an extremely uncertain time. 'If we're just sitting here and doing nothing, we're killing ourselves slowly,' he said. 'In the next ten years, either we win something back or it's going to get worse. We don't know. This is a huge gamble.'

*

The fall of the Youngspiration lawmakers was as meteoric as their rise. Just over two months after they were elected and were due to begin their duties, Baggio Leung and Yau Wai-ching were disqualified by a High Court judge who said that they had failed to take their oath of office faithfully. The verdict came a week after China's National People's Congress, which has ultimate authority over the Hong Kong courts, issued a ruling that anyone promoting separatism in Hong Kong must be barred from public office. The outcome was a surprise to no-one, given the manner of their swearing-in ceremony and the carefully orchestrated propaganda campaign against them. Looking sullen as they faced the press outside the court together, Yau described the outcome as 'not fair but expected' because of the 'threats to the judge' from Beijing. Leung said it was now clear for all to see that 'elections in Hong Kong are meaningless'. Perhaps that was what they had been trying to show all along.

Some opposition lawmakers in Hong Kong had, in the past, used their oath-taking ceremony – when they must swear allegiance to the Hong Kong Special Administrative Region of the People's Republic of China – as a chance to voice their resistance to the territory's undemocratic system. In this highly symbolic circumstance, most were allowed to get away with it. Leung and Yau, a 25-year-old with a penchant for spicy language, decided to see how far they could push this. As they took their oaths at the start of October, both unfurled banners that read 'Hong Kong is not China'. They also deliberately mispronounced China to sound like 'Chee-na', a derogatory term for the nation that was used by the Japanese during the Second World War and beforehand. Yau went even further, referring to the mother country as the 'People's Refucking of China'. Such childish actions did not merit too strong a reaction at first. Little did they know that the Beijing and Hong Kong governments sensed a chance to act decisively against the growing separatist movement and send a warning about the high costs of trying to emulate the likes of Leung and Yau.

Officials decided that they had to oust Leung and Yau, either through Hong Kong's British-style legal system or using the nuclear option of a ruling by the Chinese parliament. In the end, they did both. Just as importantly, the Liaison Office and the many pro-Beijing front groups in Hong Kong also mobilised a public campaign to vilify Leung and Yau. Many Hong Kongers, including some young people who voted for the Youngspiration duo, were disappointed by their actions. Partly because they found their comments about China offensive and partly because they had given the authorities an opportunity to kick them out, depriving their voters of a voice. The pro-Beijing front groups stirred the pot further, deploying language that echoed the denouncements of Mao Zedong's Cultural Revolution.

Normally staid organisations such as the Chinese Banking Association of Hong Kong and the Plastic Products Merchants United Association filled the press with vituperative advertisements attacking the newly elected legislators over their support for independence. A youth association said they had 'darkness and dirt in their hearts'. A group of education and cultural heavy-weights called for the pair to be banished from Hong Kong. The Hong Kong branch of the All-China Women's Federation said Yau had not just 'insulted the nation' but 'hurt the emotions of all Chinese people in the world' as well as 'losing face for all Hong Kong women'.[12]

Several months later, I caught up with Baggio Leung in central Hong Kong on a chilly winter morning. Dressed in tapered jeans, a black v-neck t-shirt and a fur-lined hoodie, with a tote bag slung over his shoulder, it was hard to imagine that this was one of the most hated people in China. Leung had dispensed with the lensless glasses that he wore while politicking to make him look more authoritative. Not wearing his signature glasses made it harder for people to recognise him now and reduced the chances of him being accosted in the street. I wanted to know why he and Yau had gone through all the hard work of the election only to risk get-ting kicked out because of the oaths.

'I wanted to show that the rule of law is not work-ing in Hong Kong any more,' he said. 'It's not about my point of view. I'm representing a group of people in Hong Kong and they need someone to push the line for them.' What about those young people who voted for them in the hope that they would fight their corner in the Legislative Council? Had they not let them down? Leung was philosophical and argued that if the government had failed in its bid to remove them, they would be seen as 'heroes'. Too many Hong Kongers care only about the result and not the fight, he said. 'We like winners. It's in our DNA. But now we're losing.'

Their situation could get worse. The young pair is appealing against their disqualification and face legal costs of millions of Hong Kong dollars for a case they almost certainly cannot win. The Legislative Council is also trying to force them to return the nearly HK$1 million each they received in salary and office set-up expenses during their short stint as lawmakers. Leung admits that there is a good chance he will be forced to go bankrupt. Neither he nor Yau will find it easy to get decent jobs, with many Hong Kong and international companies likely to shun them for fear of upsetting Beijing and the local establishment.

The next major battle, he said, will be on the streets again, not in the legal or political system. The separatists will succeed eventually, he insisted, but they need time. Leung believes that the vast majority of students in Hong Kong already support some form of self-determination or independence. But reaching out beyond this core to the rest of Hong Kong will take years. Leung thinks that timing is the other key, suggesting that another surprise movement like Occupy or unexpected changes in China could propel their struggle further forward.

'Everything planned in Hong Kong will fail', he added, laughing. 'My phone and email are all hacked by the authorities so if you have a proposal, it's better if you don't tell me.' In the end, Leung argued, Hong Kongers will see that China's Communist leaders will never give Hong Kong democracy because anything that constrains their power is a threat. Even those who remain pro-Beijing will be forced to re-examine their position as the encroachments on Hong Kong's freedoms intensify.

At his oath-taking, his controversial banner read 'Hong Kong is not China'. Now, with booksellers kidnapped by Mainland security agents, elected legislators ousted at the behest of China and political activists and their families under threat, Leung lamented that 'Hong Kong is not Hong Kong anymore'.

Fighting Back

In researching this book, I spoke to a wide range of exceptional young Hong Kongers who are on the front lines of a battle to define themselves, their city and their future at a time of great uncertainty and change.

From millionaire tutors to the leaders of the Umbrella Revolution and from the children of tycoons to iconoclastic artists, they are not meant to be a representative sample of Hong Kongers. Yet my conversations with these outspoken individuals shine a light on the conflicts and contradictions facing this important global city and the people who will be among its future leaders. Their struggle to find an accommodation – both political and personal – with the authoritarian Beijing government is indicative of the challenge that the rest of the world faces from a rising great power that is no longer willing to abide by Deng Xiaoping's call to 'hide your strength and bide your time'.

The semi-autonomy granted to Hong Kong in 1997 was always a messy compromise, designed to ensure effective Chinese control without completely alienating the local population. In the twenty years since the handover, this compromise has come under ever greater strain for a number of reasons.

Firstly, the China of Xi Jinping is a very different country to that of Jiang Zemin and Hu Jintao. Having consolidated personal power more aggressively than any leader since Mao Zedong, Xi is willing and able to wield his authority and is determined to demonstrate that the 'great rejuvenation' of the Chinese nation cannot be derailed. Secondly, the economic balance between Beijing and Hong Kong has changed dramatically because of the rapid growth of China over the last two decades. In 1997, Beijing still needed to treat Hong Kong with kid gloves because it generated nearly a fifth of the economic activity in the rest of China and was a vital bridge to the outside world in terms of trade and investment. Now Hong Kong's economy is similar in size to the neighbouring cities of Guangzhou and Shenzhen. Lastly, Hong Kong itself has changed. One of the few things that both pro-Beijing and pro-democracy supporters agree on is that many young people in Hong Kong feel very little, if any, allegiance to China. From Baggio Leung to Lau Ming-wai, Generation HK grew up thinking that they were first and foremost Hong Kongers. The democrats see this attitude through the lens of Hong Kong's values, which are unique within China, chiefly respect for the rule of law and freedom of speech. Regime backers see this generational shift as a failure by the government to ensure that Hong Kongers were properly educated about their place within China. There was, they believe, far too much focus on 'Two Systems' and not enough on 'One Country'.

Either way, the contradictions of the 1997 settlement were always likely to unwind. Maintaining a free city inside one of the world's most powerful authoritarian states is fraught with difficulties. It is not just about politics and economics. More importantly, and often overlooked, is the question of identity.

Many people and nations define themselves against 'others'. The Scottish see themselves as (most definitely) not English, the Canadians as not American and the Indonesians and Singaporeans as not Malaysian. Young Hong Kongers growing up in a vibrant city with its own language, culture and freedoms feel that they too are different, different from China. So far, the attempts by the Beijing and Hong Kong governments to crack down on the growing feeling of separateness – and separatism – have only succeeded in giving succour to the movement. Whatever happens on the political front, the authorities cannot simply brainwash a generation or two of people who have grown up feeling differently about who they are.

Political events in Hong Kong have moved so fast over the last few years that academic researchers are only just starting to make sense of them. In one such preliminary study, Brian Fong of the Education University of Hong Kong argues that Beijing's efforts to integrate Hong Kongers into China by exercising greater political, economic and ideological control 'are leading to a rise of peripheral nationalism in the city-state and waves of counter-mobilization'. He compares the situation in Hong Kong to Scotland and Catalonia, where past efforts by the British and Spanish governments respectively to combat independence and exert central government power have backfired badly.[13]

In a sign of Beijing's failure to win over young Hong Kongers and its dismay at this outcome, the Chinese government has started routinely denouncing 'Hong Kong independence' in the same way that it has denounced 'Taiwan independence' for years – despite the fact that the island of Taiwan is de facto independent. The growth of a separate Hong Kong identity, in fact, mirrors the growth of a Taiwanese identity, distinct from the ethnic Chinese background of the vast majority of the inhabitants of Taiwan and Hong Kong. China can forcibly curb Hong Kong's autonomy and, by threat of force, prevent Taiwan from formally declaring independence. However, its ever-tougher approach to both places will never win it public support.

For many members of Generation HK, the growing tensions between China and Hong Kong have crystallised the feeling that their home has its own unique character that needs to be protected. Lau Ming-wai, the billionaire property tycoon and government adviser, and Edward Leung, the radical independence advocate, both believe that Hong Kong is a special place, with a culture and political freedoms that should be defended. But, faced with a powerful master in Beijing and a divided society at home, they disagree fundamentally on how best to do so.

The dynamics of the relationship between Hong Kong and the Chinese government will continue to play a critical role as the members of Generation HK explore their identity. As they grow up, we can expect their sense of identity to drift with the tide of history in a city that is positioned between two worlds of freedom and control. With the clock ticking down to 2047, the struggle to define what it means to be a Hong Konger will intensify. At a time when many politicians and commentators around the world are lamenting the apathy of the young, Generation HK is defying stereotypes by standing up, raising its voice and fighting back.

NOTES

All websites last accessed on 14 April 2017.

1 Woodward, K. (1997) *Concepts of Identity and Difference*. In: *Identity and Difference*. UK: Sage Publications Ltd. Pp. 7-61.

2 Laclau, E. (1990) *New Reflections on the Revolution of Our Time*. London: Verso.

3 Anderson, B. (1983) *Imagined Communities: Reflections on the Origin and Spread of Nationalism*. London: Verso.

4 Transcript of Chinese Foreign Ministry press conference, 17 November 2016. http://www.fmprc.gov.cn/mfa_eng/xwfw_665399/s2510_665401/2511_665403/t1416290.shtml

5 'Watch out for Joshua Wong's new-found friends in Washington', *South China Morning Post*, 19 November 2016. http://www.scmp.com/comment/insight-opinion/article/2047436/watch-out-joshua-wongs-new-found-friends-washington

6 Documents reviewed by author and cited here: https://www.ft.com/content/b57ea50a-cfec-11e5-92a1-c5e23ef99c77

7 Figures cited by author: https://www.ft.com/content/ab819890-7232-11e5-a129-3fcc4f641d98

8 Introducing Hong Kong's 'umbrella soldiers', *BBC News*, 23 November 2015. http://www.bbc.com/news/world-asia-34897403

9 'State newspaper says dystopian HK film 'Ten Years' is ridiculous and promotes desperation', *Hong Kong Free Press*, 22 January 2016. https://www.hongkongfp.com/2016/01/22/state-newspaper-says-dystopian-hk-film-ten-years-is-ridiculous-and-promotes-desperation/

10 'Then they came for the bookseller', *Los Angeles Review of Books*,

9 January 2016. https://lareviewofbooks.org/article/then-they-came-for-the-bookseller/

11 'China introduces film industry law', *Xinhua*, 7 November 2016. http://news.xinhuanet.com/english/2016-11/07/c_135812127.html

12 'Hong Kong activists face Beijing propaganda treatment', *Financial Times*, 24 October 2016. https://www.ft.com/content/2707638e-96a7-11e6-a80e-bcd69f323a8b

13 *'One Country, Two Nationalisms: Center-Periphery Relations between Mainland China and Hong Kong, 1997–2016'*, Modern China, 2017.

ACKNOWLEDGEMENT

Many people helped with the research for this, my first book, and I am deeply grateful for their encouragement, support and insights. Rather than risk omitting anyone, I would prefer simply to thank all the contacts, colleagues and friends who assisted me as I tried to make sense of the remarkable changes roiling Hong Kong. A journalist is only as good as their sources.

PENGUIN
SPECIALS

The Inaugural Hong Kong Series

Hong Kong has many faces: international financial hub, home of martial arts films and cantopop, intercultural melting pot, former Crown colony and now Special Administrative Region of the People's Republic of China. When the United Kingdom transferred sovereignty over Hong Kong to China on 1 July 1997, the event not only ended 156 years of British rule, it also opened a new chapter of cultural, linguistic and political exploration. Twenty years later, Penguin Random House launches the Hong Kong Specials series. Seven outstanding literary and intellectual voices from Hong Kong take stock of the city as it is today, a city that has undergone an era of unforeseeable transition and at the same time is in the midst of forging a new identity.

Read more from these authors in the series:

Xu Xi
Antony Dapiran
Dung Kai-cheung
Simon Cartledge
Ben Bland
Christopher DeWolf
Magnus Renfrew

PENGUIN
SPECIALS

Dear Hong Kong

XU XI

**Let us begin here with once upon this time, at
this moment of writing an epistolary heartbreak . . .**

Xu Xi's body of work witnesses her turbulent love affair with her
home-city of Hong Kong. In this probing memoir, she unravels her
recently finalised decision to leave the city for good. She critiques a
Hong Kong that has, in her eyes, lost its way. And yet, it is only out of
the city's enduring presence in her life, both in the form of memory and
periodic homecomings, that she has carved out a personal and literary
identity. *Dear Hong Kong* is a profound reflection on the life of Hong
Kong, personified and interrogated by one of its most lucid writers.

Xu Xi is a novelist, short story writer and author of creative non-fiction
based in Hong Kong and New York. She addresses issues of the Chinese
family, diaspora and contemporary cross-cultural life in her work. She
has won the O. Henry Prize and has been shortlisted for the Man Asian
Literary Prize.

'One of [Hong Kong]'s pioneering English authors'
CNN

'Her transnational background gives her insights into the impact that
shifting geopolitics and intertwining cultures have on individual lives.'
Asia Literary Review

'Xu Xi is undoubtedly one of Hong Kong's foremost English
language writers'
Cha Asian Literary Journal

PENGUIN
SPECIALS

Borrowed Spaces

CHRISTOPHER DEWOLF

Life Between the Cracks of Modern Hong Kong

Where have all the fishballs gone? From a journalist deeply attuned to the subtleties of Hong Kong life comes *Borrowed Spaces*, a chronicle of the ways in which the grassroots citizens of Hong Kong reshape their city to make up for the shortcomings of their bureaucratic government. Mango trees sprouting on roundabouts, fishball stalls and neon signs: these are just some of the Hong Kong icons that are casualties in the struggle to reclaim public spaces. Christopher DeWolf explores the history of Hong Kong's urban growth through the daily tug of war between the people's needs to express themselves and government regulations.

Christopher DeWolf is a Hong Kong-based journalist and long-time contributor to *The Wall Street Journal* and the *South China Morning Post*. His writing has also appeared in *TIME* magazine, *The Guardian* and *Design Anthology*. Additionally, he is the managing editor for the arts, culture and history magazine *Zolima*.